The View
from Hadrian's Wall

The View from Hadrian's Wall

*Two Friends Hike Along
the Ancient Roman Frontier*

MARK CLEGG *and*
DAVID WILMOT

Toplight

Jefferson, North Carolina

LIBRARY OF CONGRESS CATALOGUING-IN-PUBLICATION DATA

Names: Clegg, Mark, 1958– author. | Wilmot, David, 1960– author.
Title: The view from Hadrian's Wall : two friends hike along
the ancient Roman frontier / Mark Clegg and David Wilmot.
Description: Jefferson, North Carolina : Toplight, 2022 |
Includes bibliographical references and index.
Identifiers: LCCN 2021050702 | ISBN 9781476685069 (paperback : acid free paper) ∞
ISBN 9781476644325 (ebook)
Subjects: LCSH: Walls, Roman—England, Northern. | Hiking—England—
Hadrian's Wall. | Hadrian's Wall (England)—Description and travel. |
Great Britain—History—Roman period, 55 B.C.–449 A.D. | BISAC: SPORTS
& RECREATION / Hiking | HISTORY / Ancient / Rome
Classification: LCC DA146 .C54 2021 | DDC 936.1/04—dc23/eng/20211110
LC record available at https://lccn.loc.gov/2021050702

BRITISH LIBRARY CATALOGUING DATA ARE AVAILABLE

ISBN (print) 978–1–4766–8506–9
ISBN (ebook) 978–1–4766–4432–5

Front cover: Sycamore Gap tree at night silhouetted by the northern lights
in Northumberland near Hadrian's Wall, United Kingdom
(Shutterstock/Christopher Chambers)

Printed in the United States of America

Toplight is an imprint of McFarland & Company, Inc., Publishers

*Box 611, Jefferson, North Carolina 28640
www.toplightbooks.com*

Table of Contents

Preface by Mark Clegg   1

Introduction by Mark Clegg   3

Introduction by David Wilmot   8

Chapter 1. Geordieland   15

Chapter 2. The Red Lion   59

Chapter 3. Moorlands   84

Chapter 4. Cumbria   133

Chapter 5. Carlisle   150

Chapter 6. Last Leg   162

Postscript   179

Chapter Notes   187

Bibliography   193

Index   195

*Old men who have followed the Eagles since boyhood
say nothing in the Empire is more wonderful than
the first sight of the Wall!*
—Rudyard Kipling, *Puck of Pook's Hill*

Candidum amicum glandem!
—David Wilmot

Preface
by Mark Clegg

I hate the term "bucket list," but that overused expression best describes my decision to finally hike the length of Hadrian's Wall in September of 2019. I needed a change of pace from sporadic hiking adventures—I had recently completed the first 500 miles of the Appalachian Trail and wanted to attempt something entirely different.

I have long been fascinated by Hadrian's Wall. Nearly 2,000 years after the Romans built it, much of the land that surrounds it continues to be remote and sparsely populated. Although I had lived in England for three years in the mid–1990s, I rarely ventured out to the far north of England, the border country region that "the Wall" snakes through as it winds its way from the North Sea to the Irish Sea.

A lengthy hike represents a holistic experience—there is, first and foremost, the sheer physical challenge of walking 15, 20, and even 25 miles per day. The rigors of such hikes are always a shock—I typically do not have the time available to train for the harsh impact that multi-day treks inflict on my body.

I have always been a believer in "hiking with history"—researching the areas that will be traversed to discover their relevance to the distant past and their lingering influence on current events. Hadrian's Wall provided a rich seam of material to consider not only ancient Rome's influence on modern-day Britain but also how many of the same symptoms of the Roman Empire's decline are now manifesting themselves in the Anglosphere of both Britain and America.

Preface by Mark Clegg

A hike always represents an opportunity for chance encounters with people whom one would ordinarily never meet in everyday life. Their views, culture, food and drink and captivating dialects are an endless source of fascination.

Finally, this book is about renewed friendship. Dave and I had not met or talked to each other for 15 years prior to our decision—agreed to in a brief email exchange—to hike the Wall, an idea that we had never discussed during the 10-year active phase of our friendship. In one of those wonderful moments of serendipity, it somehow made perfect sense in that stage of our lives in 2019 for us to meet up and hike the length of Hadrian's Wall.

My editor at Toplight made the suggestion that the book represent "two voices," wherein both Dave and I would record our observations along the hike, memories of our past, and concerns about the future. While initially skeptical, I believe that this approach enriches the story and adds perspective from both an English and an American viewpoint.

My contribution is in regular roman text (and standard American English). Dave Wilmot's is in *italics* and uses British English.

All events recorded along the hike are real, although we have sometimes changed the names of individuals we met in order to respect their privacy.

This book has been extensively researched, and all applicable sources are cited in both the chapter notes and bibliography.

Introduction
by Mark Clegg

My first glimpse of England was in 1989 from the beaches of Calais in France. On that mid–October day, my wife and I could just make out the fabled White Cliffs of Dover across the 30-mile-wide English Channel.

This was a good five years before the "Chunnel" was built, linking France to Britain via high-speed trains that sped at more than 100 miles per hour deep below the Straits of Dover. The preferred method of cross-channel travel in those days was the hovercraft, an inflatable amphibious vessel that produced a super-charged air cushion just below its surface, which allowed it to glide over the choppy, gray waters of the North Sea in just half an hour.

Our fellow passengers were largely English vacationers who had prepared for the brief voyage by tanking up on cheap lager at one of the numerous French "hypermarkets" that sold duty-free beer. Their celebratory mood was infectious, and I felt the excitement building as we skimmed over the channel towards the Kentish coast.

After landing in Dover, we exited the hovercraft and began schlepping our luggage in the general direction of town. A fog had blown in from the sea, and a "bobby," a British policeman, emerged from the thick mist. It was a scene so cliché that it would have never made it past the cutting room floor of any movie, but the friendly cop, walking calmly with his arms folded behind his back, cheerfully gave us directions to our mid-century motel on Snargate Street.

Over the next 10 days, we explored the traditional tourist haunts in the south of England, as far west as Salisbury and Dorchester, then up north to Bath and Oxford, before heading back south to London. We spent our evenings in affordable family-owned inns or bed and breakfasts in centuries-old towns surrounded by huge swatches of rolling greensward, seemingly occupied by nothing but legions of Southdown and Cotswold sheep.

This was before the chain and box stores had steamrolled so many small business owners, thereby removing much of the charm of the towns and villages in both England and America. It was still a time of independent bookstores, scruffy newsagents, family-owned teashops, pubs and butchers. Each speck on the map had a sense of place, a fierce hold on its unique and timeless heritage that it could treasure for its past, if not its future.

It was not all ideal during that era 30 years ago—this was well before culinary choices had exploded in Britain and the meal alternatives were typically either tandoori chicken, a desultory potted meat and cucumber sandwich or some other form of traditional English fare. It felt like haute cuisine when a wedge of lemon was offered with mushy peas and fish and chips.

But the mediocre food, combined with the much-derided weather, added to the sense of distinctiveness—there are always tradeoffs, and I gladly accepted these shortcomings in exchange for the carefully protected history, the gentle beauty of the West Country, the stark splendor of the Yorkshire Dales, and the low-key charms of London, as cosmopolitan as any city in the world, but not nearly as manic as New York or Hong Kong.

My wife and I moved to South Kensington in London in the mid–1990s, and our daughter was born in the borough of Westminster. A polite but no-nonsense clerk recorded her birth in a dusty, leather-bound registry in longhand cursive. We left Britain in 1996, just before "Cool Britannia," English Premier League soccer, the Spice Girls, and Austin Powers seeped into the world's consciousness. Our time there was, in many ways, a bridge between two eras—Britain was just beginning to shed the last remnants of its imperial past and was embracing a modern and open future, which culminated in the vibrant and universally acclaimed 2012 London Olympics.

The subsequent twin seismic political events of 2016—the June vote by Britain to leave the European Union, followed by the November election of Donald Trump in America—reinvigorated my interest in the links between our two countries. In retrospect, the Brexit vote was the proverbial "canary in the coal mine" to the stunning populist revolt that manifested itself in the American presidential election.

My interest in Roman history was kindled by my experience as an exchange student in Cologne in the 1970s—the Roman museum next to the iconic Gothic cathedral and sections of the original Roman city wall that cropped up in the "Altstadt" were reminders of how an ancient Mediterranean power made deep inroads into the wilds of northern Europe.

I have also long been interested in the history of Britain, particularly the Roman period that lasted more than 400 years. London, like Cologne, had a Roman city wall that surrounded what is today's financial district, and it stood, basically intact, for about 1,700 years. The fortunate areas in Europe that could lay claim to Roman heritage proudly did so—I remember one of my English colleagues in London sniffing, "if the Romans didn't build roads on it, it's not civilized." This caustic comment was made as a putdown of the "Celtic Fringe" of Wales, Scotland, and Ireland.

I was fascinated by the relics of the Roman past displayed in London museums—the helmets, armor, and shields, which had been preserved for centuries while buried in peat bogs or airless river bottom mud. I managed, just before we left Britain to move back to the United States, to visit the best-known vestige of Britain's Roman past—a section of Hadrian's Wall near Carlisle.

For fast-paced historical fiction, I devoured the novels of Jack Whyte and Bernard Cornwell that touched on the history of the Wall. I read (and have used as source material for this book) numerous works detailing the history of the Roman presence in Britain.

In the aftermath of 2016, articles and books began to appear drawing parallels between the collapse of the Roman Republic and the cracks that were beginning to spread among the foundations of the democratic West. To varying degrees, these comparisons were both fascinating and concerning.

Early in 2019, I reached out to an old English friend whom I had not seen in 15 years to walk the length of Hadrian's Wall. I offered him the option to respond "hell no!" should he find the idea repugnant. I expected either a deafening silence to my proposal or a typically polite English demurral. Surprisingly, his almost immediate "hell yes!" signified his buy-in to the notion of venturing into "the personal unknown of traversing my country by foot." Hiking Hadrian's Wall was something which he had not thought about since his youth, and while somewhat intimidated from a physical perspective, he admitted to a compulsion driven by the Wall's sheer historical and physical stature. In his words, he had to do it "because it was there." After adding in the novelty of what was to be literally a cross-country walk, there was, simply put, "no more thinking to be done." A plan was hatched, and we agreed to meet up and hike the "Path," while sharing laughs, drinks, stories from our past, and concerns about the future.

My comments, thoughts, and observations are represented in plain text. *Dave's appear in italics.* While my comments and observations are written in standard American English, Dave's remarks reflect conventional "Queen's English" such as "centre," "whilst," and "humour." His spelling of words such as "organise" and "recognise" also mirror standard British English.

The terms Scots, Picts, Caledonians and Celts are used somewhat interchangeably in this book to describe the tribes north of Hadrian's Wall. What we now refer to as Scots were actually in Ireland at the time Hadrian's Wall was built; Picts were first recorded in written Roman records in 297 CE; and Caledonians refer to the nine Celtic tribes identified by the Romans at the time the Wall was built. The genetic pool of modern-day Scotland reflects the rich influence of all these peoples.

England, Scotland, Wales, and Northern Ireland make up the modern United Kingdom. Great Britain (Britain) consists of all these countries with the exception of Northern Ireland. Britannia was the name given to the Roman province south of Hadrian's Wall.

References to dates are "BCE" (Before Common Era) and "CE" (Common Era), which have largely supplanted the use of BC and AD in contemporary scholarship.

Introduction
by David Wilmot

From an early age, living in England brings one into contact with the history of the Roman invasion and occupation of these shores, and the permanent legacy which they left behind after their departure at the beginning of the 5th century CE. I was born in the city of Gloucester in the southwest of England and was aware as a youngster that our city was called Glevum during Roman times. The more formal name is Colonia Nervia Glevensium with this passage of history commemorated by a statue of the Emperor Nerva in modern-day Gloucester. Similarly, my parents and siblings are from the city of Exeter, which sits on the site of Isca Dumnoniorum, a Roman army fortress that was established in 55 CE, the original walls of which exist to this day as part of the medieval city walls. These are just two examples of the plethora of towns and cities in Great Britain that have Roman origins. Easily the most spectacular is the city of Bath (or "Aquae Sulis"), with its Roman temple, and the Roman bath house with its geothermally heated water supply naturally pumping up rainwater from the nearby Mendip Hills. As if visits to Bath require any additional attractions, the city boasts one of England's most successful rugby teams, which plays in a wonderful setting in the city's stunningly well-preserved Georgian centre.

Not surprisingly, school trips regularly involved excursions to Roman places of interest as my school did its best to put my classmates and me in touch with our ancient history. As a youngster, I spent a fair proportion of my time glued to the TV watching a seemingly endless succession of Westerns and movies depicting various historical events. In particular, films and documentaries depicting the Roman Empire were genuinely exciting, and it was inspirational to be able to walk and sometimes run around amongst the actual physical relics of those ancient bygone times. One such example was a school visit to Maiden Castle in Dorset, one of the largest Iron Age hill forts in Britain, believed to have been established in 800 BCE. The fortress was still occupied by Celts at the time of the Roman invasion of Britain in 43 CE, and we were told about the 2nd Legion Augusta under their leader (and later emperor) Vespasian, who was believed to have led an assault upon the castle. The mythology of this was reinforced by the discovery in the 1930s of the remains of more than 52 skeletons, believed to be warriors of the Celtic Durotriges tribe, buried with beads, brooches and rings as well as their weapons in the grounds of the fort.

From Maiden Castle, our school group made its way to a nearby campsite, where we were to spend the next week trying to co-exist under canvas in "ridge tents," some of which appeared so old that they could easily have seen active service in World War II. We arrived still quite animated about the visit to Maiden Castle and the scenario imparted to us by our teachers of the battle between its occupants and the Romans. We were probably acting out our own Roman battles, inspired by the likes of Kirk Douglas in the 1960 movie Spartacus. Unfortunately, we soon found that some of the other schools staying at the camp had some older boys amongst them who seemed to be running the camp along Roman military lines and who would intimidate us on a daily basis. I am happy to admit now that we dealt successfully with this by presenting a constant moving target, never staying in one area of the camp long enough for them to give us a proper Lord of the Flies–style thrashing, and never under any circumstances to go anywhere near the washing facilities where they would be able to corner us. Whilst this strategy spared us from the threat of a "duffing over" by the older schoolboys, it did mean that we went for a week washing *in streams or from standpipes and probably were not that pleasant to be anywhere in the vicinity of. Upon our return to Gloucester and safety, my mother, spotting me from a distance descending the steps of our coach, was quizzical as to why I was wearing gloves in the height of the glorious summer of 1970. Upon closer observation of a number of us, she realized that my "gloves" and generally disheveled state in fact betrayed the only very rudimentary ablutions, which we had been forced to take for the sake of our self-preservation.*

I guess that a takeaway from this violence-avoidance episode is that I probably would not have been much use as Roman legionary. But the fascination with this era of history, the culture and its physical legacy around the UK remained. The study of Shakespeare's Roman plays at school succeeded in bringing some of the history to life albeit my one school visit from our new home in Lancashire to the great Bard's birthplace in Stratford is more remembered for my first (as a 14-year-old) experience of drinking in pubs rather than any academic enrichment.

In the initial years of senior school, the study of Latin was mandatory, but I stuck with it later on when it became optional. My choice was between studying Latin and Chemistry, and although my decision to study the former subject was partly driven by a deep desire to sidestep any involvement with the latter, I soon realized that I had struck gold. I found it a beautiful language with the clear linkage with English words often enabling the intuitive derivation of the meaning of Latin words without necessitating the use of dictionaries. From a purely academic perspective, my involvement with Latin ceased when I was 16 after completing my O Level exams, but my appreciation of its central place in the construction of the English language continued. I experienced a somewhat amusing example of this only a few years ago whilst visiting my son, who was studying at the University of Alicante in the Costa Blanca region of southeastern Spain. We took the train to the city of Valencia where we watched a soccer match in Spain's La Liga between Valencia CF and Sevilla FC. The game was staged at Valencia's imposing Mestalla stadium. The

Mestalla has a seating capacity of 48,600 with vertiginously steep stands, and we found it to be the home of some of the most passionate and voluble supporters we had ever encountered. On the way into this sporting amphitheatre, walking past the bar area selling excellent if fully-priced Estrella beer and pizzas, we noticed a large sign bearing the legend "Vomitorio" on the wall of the passageway leading into the main stadium. When we are together our humour standards usually descend at some point to schoolboy level and we immediately wondered if this was a haven for fans who had taken on rather too much of the cervezas and were feeling ill. Once we had managed to get this gratuitous gag out of our systems, I felt that it could only mean one thing and again it made perfectly good sense—the Latin word "vomitorium" relates to a passageway in Ancient Roman amphitheatres through which large crowds can exit rapidly at the end of the performance, literally "spewing forth" from the stadium. It was the first time we had come across this appellation for what we would call a passageway or a gangway, but it made intuitive sense and reminded me how I love the way that the context in which Latin words can immediately point to their English meaning. We later learned that the Oregon Shakespeare Festival has vomitoria in two of its theaters, which are colloquially referred to as "the voms," although I have to confess to a strong preference for the original longer Latin version.

So, as John Cleese questioned as the character Reg in Monty Python's Life of Brian *after the Romans took so much from us, "what have they ever given us in return?" After some back and forth with his cohorts concluding that the Romans were way ahead of most of civilization, Reg floats the challenge to his confounded colleagues. "All right, but apart from the sanitation, the medicine, education, wine, public order, irrigation, roads, a fresh water system and public health what have the Romans ever done for us?" The same applies with the contribution that they made in Britain. Despite the way they treated our Iron Age ancestors during the occupation of Britain, the Romans, both physically and culturally, had an indelible influence upon what we grew into as a country. The physical relics, the cultural references,*

Above and opposite: **Map of the Hike Along Hadrian's Wall (provided by Kendall Young of WoodBatBrand.com).**

and the origins of language are there for all to see and continue to attract our interest two millennia further on.

For all of the historical remains of the Roman occupation of Britain and the enjoyment I have experienced in visiting them, there really is no experience of this that comes close to visiting the Foro Romano and the Colosseum in Rome. Having visited it several times,

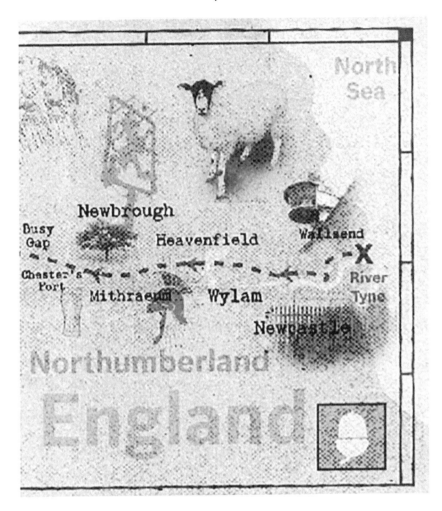

I'm still amazed that it has survived so well, almost like a skeletal version of a modern sporting arena. In its original form it could hold up to 80,000 spectators and had 80 vomitoria, considerably more, I would venture, than there are at the Mestalla in Valencia. During my first visit to Rome with my wife, I also made visits to the adjacent and equally captivating Foro Romano and then to the Caracalla Baths where the "Three Tenors," Placido Domingo, Jose Carreras and Luciano Pavarotti, performed their legendary concert in July 1990

---

before the FIFA World Cup was staged in Italy. By the time we had completed our visits to these breathtaking landmarks, it felt that no other Roman experiences could bear comparison. They probably cannot—but in my book, participation will always beat spectating and walking the entire length of Hadrian's Wall would provide a different and energizing kind of experience and challenge.

Any interest in Roman heritage naturally brings with it an awareness of Hadrian's Wall, but prior to Mark's suggestion that we should walk it together, the possibility of doing it had never really entered my thoughts. I was aware that quite large sections of the Wall were still intact and that it passed through some quite magnificent and rugged countryside, but my travels either rarely took me anywhere near any part of it or we simply drove straight past its environs without any second thoughts on our journeys to and from my wife's birthplace in Edinburgh. But Mark's call and suggestion came at the right moment and there were a number of reasons why an East-West traversing of England held a strong allure for me at that time. The opportunity to spend time with my old friend, reminisce about shared experiences and get some terrific exercise walking the Path all made sense. There was another motivation—that of taking a time-out to almost "look back" at the UK and where we are heading and make some sense of my disappointment at our enforced distancing from Continental Europe resulting from the European Union referendum and the inexorable progression towards our leaving the Union or "Brexit," as it has come to be known. So it was time to take a breather from my professional life in London, bid a loving à bientot *to my family and take a trip up to the north of England to conduct what for me was a completely new experience—that of hiking through history and the unknown.*

CHAPTER 1

Geordieland

Our train from London slid slowly into Newcastle upon Tyne in the early evening on the next to the last day of summer in 2019. In service since 1850, the Victorian era railway station had wrought iron ribs, which supported a curved roof with glass panels extending out on both sides of its apex. The last rays of the sun gleamed through the glass, strewing light and shadow along the length of the platform.

I had met up with Dave the previous day and spent the evening with him and his family in the leafy south London borough of Kew Gardens. He had been my closest English friend when my wife, daughter, and I lived in London during the mid–1990s. We had not seen or talked to each other since my last visit to England in 2004, but as is always the case with old friends, we had no problem picking up where we left off. The conversations ranged from the respective contemporary political landscapes of our home countries, the UK's current obsession with artisanal gins and mixers, and our memories of working with a collection of colorful and in some cases bizarre individuals at a Canadian bank in London 25 years ago. We had spent much of the time the previous evening and the morning catching up and chuckling over the prospect of two sixtyish and out of shape old friends heading to the north of England, to hike Hadrian's Wall.

We had also spent an enjoyable hour at Kew's Good Wine Shop, with Ben, the affable proprietor, who hailed from Sunderland, just south of Newcastle. As a native of Sunderland, Ben is technically a "Mackem" (pronunciation rhymes with "crack-em") rather than a "Geordie," the affectionate term used to describe those from Newcastle

*and its environs. The derivation of the Mackem ethnonym is not
wholly clear but is believed to have its roots in Sunderland's history
in the now largely defunct shipbuilding industry on Wearside—i.e.,
"we mack 'em and ye tack 'em" or "we make the ships and you take the
ships."*[1]

Ben possessed an encyclopedic knowledge of beers, wines and
spirits across the northeast of England and was a great source for
places to visit en route—many more than we would have time for,
but his rough-hewn northern humour and infectious bonhomie
exemplified the warmth with which people from his region are often
associated.

*As a budding entrepreneur he must have been mightily pleased
when his shop subsequently made a fleeting appearance in BBC TV's
highly popular* Killing Eve *series. I whimsically equated the Good
Wine Shop as having the same role for Mark and me as the East India
Club for Phileas Fogg in* Around the World in Eighty Days. *We were
getting set for our departure and a journalist friend at the table next
to us assured me that he had walked sections of the Wall Path before
and that there was nothing to it. But had he, I asked myself, completed
the entire Path and had he unlike me, actually pursued lengthy outdoor walks as a pastime? The longest walk I could recall in my adult-
hood was a charity fundraiser of about six miles length over the flat,
non-threatening terrain of south London with my young son nestled in
a rucksack on my back. That, however, had been over 20 years hitherto when I somewhat misguidedly considered myself to be indestruc-
tible, and thus my concerns of not being able to hack it on the arduous
walk ahead of us remained with me as impact time got ever closer.*

I had approached Dave earlier that winter over the prospect of
hiking Hadrian's Wall, which had long been on my bucket list. When
my family and I lived in England, we traveled to the Lake District
one December, and I made a special trip just to see and stand (now
strictly forbidden) on a section of the Wall near Carlisle. Remnants
of the ancient stonewall, built almost 2,000 years ago by decree of
the Roman Emperor Hadrian, stretch for 84 miles across the narrow

east-west neck of England. Our train would arrive on a Saturday evening, and we were planning on starting our walk on Sunday morning
in Newcastle; the goal was to finish in Bowness-on-Solway the following Friday. We would be walking from the North Sea to the Irish
Sea, over and along urban landscapes, rivers, motorways, farmland,
villages, moors, and marshes.

*Whilst I had no hesitation in agreeing to join Mark, I admitted
to having had an equally immediate concern that I could comfort-
ably complete a walk covering the 84 miles across often-hilly terrain,
confronting bizarre and unexpected hazards. In recent times my only
walk involving any sort of difficult climb was the steep path up to the
spectacular views at the 3,196-foot summit of Ben Lomond, a mountain in the Scottish Highlands. Apart from that I had never done any
real rugged hiking since a not very fondly remembered series of walks
in the uplands of Lancashire and Yorkshire whilst at school. On one
particularly unpleasant excursion of the short-lived Kirkham Gram-
mar School Fell Walking Club ("fell walking" being a name given to
hill or mountain walking in Northern England), we were caught in a
blizzard on Ingleborough, one of the "Three Peaks" of Yorkshire, freez-
ing in woefully inadequate clothing. A sudden gust of wind removed a
brand new pair of glasses—to be lost forever—and my abiding memory was of a miserable long coach journey home to the Fylde coast
in Lancashire, and wondering how I would explain the loss of my
new glasses to my parents. After all, the £13 cost of the glasses, which
has been stamped on my memory ever since, didn't feel like "walking around money" in those days. My parents were characteristically
philosophical about my ocular mishap but fell-walking lost its allure
to me after that episode, and I rarely thought about it until the call
came from Mark to consider coming out of hiking exile and take on the
Wall, an unknown quantity as a physical challenge but equally in my
eyes a unique chance to venture into "real" countryside and experience an unfamiliar part of this country—one often passed on numerous visits to my wife's native Scotland, but never explored.*

In my nearly four decades of living in London, the principal mainline stations such as Euston, King's Cross, Victoria and Pad-dington came to evoke differing sentiments which had become defined by the ultimate destination and its meaning to me. Paddington, for instance, represents a gateway to my native West Country and the scenery observed from the train becomes progressively more beauti-ful as it winds through the coastal and rural stretches of Devon and Cornwall. London Victoria I associated with many visits to Brigh-ton on the South Coast and its unique drop-down menu of attrac-tions ranging from the promise of cleansing sea air to the spectacular Regency architecture of the Brighton Pavilion existing cheek-by-jowl with the area around the town's Victorian-era Palace Pier in all of its contrasting glory offering uber-garish amusement arcades and rides and chilled-out hipster coastal vibes all in the same package. Liver-pool Street Station was the portal to the bleakly beautiful and flat fenlands of East Anglia.

I have always felt this association of the train journey as a con-duit to a changed physical and emotional environment more acutely than with airports. It may have something to do with the architecture and smell of the older train stations, which have not all been modern-ized in the same way as, say, London Heathrow Airport. Whatever the reason, I know several people who make their own mental con-nections with rail travel, both good and bad. For many years I have actively looked forward to the comfort and efficiency of travelling on Deutsche Bahn's intercity routes, whereas two German acquaintances of mine have admitted to a continuing sense of foreboding in associ-ating the same journeys with having to leave their family homes in their youth to participate in mandatory military national service. For some, undoubtedly sometimes it is better to travel than to arrive.

Since I could count on one hand the number of times I had trav-eled via train in the United States for business and pleasure, my association with trains was entirely Eurocentric, usually tied to Ger-many's Deutsche Bahn. European trains always had an immediate calming effect on me. At departure, the conductor's whistle, fol-lowed by the whoosh of doors closing and the gentle release of brakes lowered my blood pressure perceptibly, especially since arriving at the train station and schlepping my luggage to the appropriate platform was typically a frantic and sweaty adventure.

Even today, I will listen to Kraftwerk's "Europa Endlos" or "Trans Europa Express" to relive the Zen-like glow I associate with gazing out the window of a speeding train as ridiculously picturesque scenery zoomed by. In particular, I remember one 17-hour train ride from Milan to Prague where I desperately fought off jet lag induced fatigue—I did not want to miss one second of a late spring journey through the Tyrolean Alps in Italy and Austria.

The train ride to Newcastle was no disappointment. I spotted, in the distance to the east, Ely Cathedral, the "Ship of the Fens," so-called because of its soaring prominence in the otherwise flat Norfolk landscape. Ripe farmlands, brimming with crops awaiting the September harvest, bordered the train track. Smaller Norman era stone churches dotted the towns whose names I can no longer recall. I loved this time of year, high in the northern latitudes, when earth approached the autumnal equinox and the haze of summer was lifting and the air assumed a lighter and clearer quality.

Legend has it that Queen Victoria for her part apparently hated Newcastle and always insisted upon a servant drawing the curtains at her train window upon approaching the city upon the Tyne. Perhaps the same journey north, which we were now taking, was one that in the 19th century had left Her Majesty distinctly "not amused." As I walked through the main concourse of King's Cross Station at the start of our journey, observing the throngs of holidaymakers queuing outside the "Harry Potter Platform 9¾" gift shop, my mind scrolled back to a previous journey north to Edinburgh to watch a Scotland vs. England Calcutta Cup rugby international. This fixture has always held a special allure for me, and I frequently made the trip to Scotland to watch it. On this occasion, in 2000, such was the apparent gulf in quality between the two teams that none of the informed commentators in the press regarded Scotland as having a realistic chance of winning the match. I felt the same way, observing how the pleasant and, on the face of it, quiescent, weather on the journey north was likely to assist England's quest to beat Scotland and win the much-coveted "Grand Slam" representing a perfect record over all of the other teams in the tournament known as the Six Nations Championship. Basking in the early afternoon sunshine pouring into my train carriage as I surveyed the gorgeous coastal stretches around Berwick-upon-Tweed, the northernmost town in Northumberland before the border with Scotland, I came across a sobering weather forecast in Scotland's national The Scotsman newspaper. To this day I think of it as the most chilling and disastrously accurate of meteorological forewarnings—predicting biblical downpours of rain and sleet the following day accompanied by the darkly partisan "Good anti–Grand Slam weather" observation of the newspaper's weather team. Sure enough, England went down in defeat the following day in a weather deluge which the Scots seemed far better suited for, and my abiding memory was of delirious kilt-wearing Scotsman running onto the pitch and performing extravagant aquaplaning, knee-first, "Klinsmann dives" whilst the majority of Murrayfield Stadium riotously celebrated the Scottish victory as the stadium public address system blasted out The Proclaimers' "500 Miles." Whilst the atmosphere at the Calcutta Cup was always lively and sometimes superficially hostile (on my first-ever visit to the stadium some victorious Scottish supporters delighted in unfurling a "Remember Bannockburn" banner in celebration of their victory on the battlefield in 1314), any anti–English sentiments only seemed to last as long as the match itself, after which supporters of both sides would socialize together well into the night. It wasn't the first time that I had experienced the crushing of my expectations of a resounding victory by my beloved English rugby team. In an email message to Mark I encapsulated the moment by characterizing another Emperor's New Clothes rugby performance as a line from a David Bowie song about "always crashing in the same car." Mark shot back with a salutary "hubris gets you every time!"

So the railway journey North from King's Cross always held that association for me, stimulating memories of the expected bacchanalian weekend at the rugby in Edinburgh amongst good friends, with the occasional twinge of dread that England's victory push may once again prove to be built on sand. It is always the hope that kills you.

This latest trip with Mark also made me think of the political and cultural environment in contemporary England. Much has been made in the press of the North-South socio-economic divide and the lack of awareness in London of the economic plight of low-income people and families in some parts of the north of England. Undoubtedly some of this dissatisfaction had worked through into the anti–European Union ("EU") movement and the ultimate outcome of the EU referendum to "Leave." To me, it felt very sad to be severing the political, and to some extent, emotional unity with a continent which I felt as much part of as the UK itself. As I peered through the window and counted off the towns and cities which had voted to "Leave"— Stevenage, Peterborough, Lincoln, Doncaster, Selby, Darlington and Gateshead all caught my attention in this context on our northbound path—I thought back to the optimism with which the UK had joined the EU in 1973. I revisited the sinking feeling that the UK had become so divided over this issue. To compound this political fragmentation, Scotland, a country I had grown to love over the past three decades now had the Scottish National Party ("SNP") as its dominant political party. Following a "No" (i.e., "Remain") vote in a 2014 Referendum to decide whether Scotland should become independent from the rest of the United Kingdom, the SNP was now using its overwhelming desire to stay within the EU as a clarion call to renew the drive for Scottish Independence with an "Indyref 2."

Following a brief flirtation with left-wing ideology in my early teens, I had become relatively apolitical. Nonetheless, the growing polarities within the UK were impossible to ignore and a sad reflection on its growing social fault lines. Put more bluntly, the UK and England that I know seemed at high risk of turning its back on its international relationships that had been the bedrock of post-war peace and prosperity. Any number of attempts at trying to convince oneself that those relationships would continue regardless of the outcome of the EU negotiations and the Scottish independence debate felt to be more grounded in hope than expectation. The outlook was uncertain and unsettling, not least for many of the younger generation who, due to the outcome of the EU referendum, now found their aspirations of working in continental Europe thrown into disarray.

I have always loved working and living in London. To me, the city has always been stimulating, challenging, cosmopolitan and endlessly changing in a good way. However, London can become all consuming both professionally and socially. The opportunity to spend a week, albeit in itinerant mode, outside of London was a big motivation and Mark's suggestion to do the walk came at a good time. I had grown progressively more frustrated at the notion of an England that had become irreversibly divided both by culture as well as wealth. I did not really buy into the idea that all Londoners "looked down their noses" at the outlying regions or that all of the occupants of provincial towns and cities were resentful of London's greater wealth, a perception which had become increasingly prevalent and often amplified by the media. At the same time I realized that I had been remote from non–London life for so long that perhaps England had changed in this way and that I had become too blinkered by the London factor to notice it. Against the backdrop of our hyperactive political environment I wondered what "England" I would find by seeing and experiencing it at first hand rather than through the metropolitan London prism. At the very least, an extended walk along Hadrian's Wall seemed like a much-needed diversion from the ceaseless and exhausting Brexit debate.

However, I continued to have uncertainties. By the end of the first day would I find myself regretting our excursion as a misguided escapade? Would my hopes be dashed and would I regret turning my back on watching England's run in the Rugby World Cup from the comfort of my London home? I had none of the answers to this and was strangely energized by the fact that I had everything still to learn. At the same time I had no idea if physically I was equal to the demands of the walk. My workouts at the local gym had certainly boosted my confidence, but I was also pragmatic enough to realize that hiking an average of over 15 miles a day over hilly and often soaked terrain would present an altogether different challenge. In a way, this lack of certainty as to whether I was doing the right thing represented in itself an attractive conundrum.

The fact that I had incomplete information to make the decision called to mind a memorable line by Orson Welles' character Michael O'Hara, an itinerant sailor in my favorite movie, The Lady from Shanghai: "I never make my mind up about anything until it's all over and done with." Like a lot of people, my professional and family life is always mapped out months in advance and could not be more diametrically opposed to Michael's. Nonetheless, there was a certain appeal to the notion of leaving my comfort zone and taking a chance on how I would enjoy life in the sometimes harsh, but unspoiled surroundings of the Hadrian's Wall Path for a few days.

Newcastle could not have provided a starker contrast to the bucolic country vistas I envisioned whose images are captured in the slick tourist guidebooks and brochures. An iconic city with a strong cultural identity, Newcastle is famous for its industrial and business heritage, its football team, irrepressible humor, and for contributions to popular culture through the decades with acts as diverse as Roxy Music, Sting, Dire Straits, and The Animals. It was twilight when we walked outside the train station—the lights from St. James' Park, home of Newcastle United Football Club shined through the gloaming. The "Magpies" of Newcastle were playing fellow Premier League bottom feeder Brighton in a match that would ultimately end in a humdrum 0–0 draw. It would be a grueling 350+ mile journey for many of the travelling Brighton "Seagulls" supporters but they could at least console themselves over the prospect of joining the "Geordies"—the nickname for citizens of Newcastle and the surrounding area of north eastern England—in what was clearly shaping up into a lively night's entertainment in the downtown area.

There are several theories about the origins of the expression

"Geordie." The most authoritative appears to be the "Geordie" safety lamps, invented by George Stephenson in 1815, which were used by local miners to prevent explosions due to firedamp (methane) in coalmines. The term distinguished the users of this lamp from the "Davy" lamp, invented by Sir Humphrey Davy at the same time, and which was used in many other collieries in the region. The spirit of the local people resonates in a quote attributed to novelist Jack Common, a native of Heaton (near Newcastle) that "Geordie goes beyond mere geography and is a quality of heart." The Newcastle University Library website also references "the quite specific belief that only people born on the North of the Tyne within 1 mile of Newcastle are entitled to call themselves 'Geordies.'"[2] I suspect that the flower of Newcastle's youth quickly assembling in the city centre that evening, undoubtedly stoked with a variety of alcoholic sustenance and ubiquitous civic pride, would not have much truck with that definition and would all regard themselves as genuine "card-carrying" Geordies regardless of their place of birth.

The Newcastle city centre's streets were alive with young people "out on the toon" (town) heading for bars and clubs and some "serious drinking." A friend of my eldest daughter who hails from the Newcastle area told her that there are two tiers of Geordie inebriation and subsequent hangover after a highly alcoholic evening—with entry level drunkenness known as "getting mortal"—or in the gold medal-winning cases "getting Voldermortal." By the looks of things on the toon that evening, some of the youngsters were heading rapidly for the Dark Lord's version of bacchanalian outcomes.

Newcastle is a city with a big personality, and with that comes various caricatured perceptions, one of which is that the men and women ("lads" and "lasses") are unusually resilient to the cold and will happily roam the streets scantily clad regardless of cryo-baric level temperature conditions. While ruminating on this subject, I recalled a Reeves and Mortimer British TV sketch where a stricken polar explorer is rescued by a young Geordie couple in skimpy night club attire who, rather than offering the traditional warming brandy *brought by a St Bernard dog, attempted to revive the explorer with a perfectly chilled six-pack of the region's legendary Newcastle Brown Ale.*

On arrival in a new city, one's frame of reference for the day or days ahead can often be set by a particularly lively exchange with local cab drivers. The most engaging and memorable ones are curious about plans for your visit to their city and just need the right spark of information about you to become opinion-machines which can sometimes leave you with a lasting impression of them and an expectation of what's ahead during your stay. I use the qualification "sometimes" here as on one visit in 2000 to Atlanta, where I was combining a business meeting with catching up with Mark, the motor-mouthed taxi driver proceeded to harp on in animated fashion about "Old Sparky," which I quickly determined to be not some kind of low-grade comic book character but instead transpired to be the electric chair at the Georgia State Prison. He told me that the chair was shortly to be decommissioned and sounded genuinely disappointed at this development.

Another inauspicious start came in Durban, South Africa, where our driver, a representative of the local Zippy Cabs service, managed to collide with a colleague's car. Enraged, he leapt out to launch into a full-on argument with its driver, leaving my friends and I wondering if this spat would escalate further and we might never get out of the multi-storey car park and realize our dream of seeing the British and Irish Lions rugby team play in South Africa.

Despite these less auspicious incidences, I have concluded from numerous experiences that my theory about cab drivers generally holds true. Once, upon arriving in Sydney on a holiday with my wife, I was quickly introduced by our driver to Australian knockabout humor, which we would encounter throughout our stay. Australia at the time was making a habit of destroying England in successive "Ashes" cricket series, prompting our driver to waggishly observe "the reassuring thing about you English is that you're so eminently beatable." I could have clarified that my wife is Scottish but I don't think that this factual counterthrust would have shaken him from his confident worldview.

On another occasion in Berlin, I was struck by my driver's bemoaning of the "Disneyfication" of his city's history and how the proliferation of museums and various tourist attractions since unification had made too light a matter of the suffering endured by thousands of families during the years of Berlin's forced division between East and West. I almost felt guilty to later visit the DDR Museum where, amongst many other attractions, one can play a game of East Germany vs. West Germany table football ("foosball") and be photographed at a Stasi-style desk backed by imposing black-and-white photographs of Karl Marx, Vladimir Lenin and Friedrich Engels—both exhibits would undoubtedly have met with the voluble Berlin cab driver's disapproval.

I was lucky enough to experience the "authentic" Berlin Wall in the summer of 1980. While studying in Germany for three months, my girlfriend and I took advantage of the one-day passes available to westerners that allowed us to walk through Checkpoint Charlie into East Berlin. The sense of gloom and paranoia was palpable on that hot August day, and our fear was heightened by the prevailing tensions of the time—the Soviet Union had recently invaded Afghanistan, the United States then promptly withdrew from the 1980 Moscow Summer Olympics games in response, and the American military had conducted a disastrous helicopter rescue attempt of its hostages held in Tehran. So, real or imagined, we felt that East German and even Soviet "watchers" were following our every move. After a desultory boiled chicken lunch washed down by watery beer at a state-owned restaurant on the Alexanderplatz and a couple of tense encounters with surly store clerks, we scampered back over the border into West Berlin, tails tucked firmly between our legs.

As Mark and I approached the taxi rank outside Newcastle Station, taking in a good lungful of the city's downtown late afternoon airs, I inwardly hoped that we would get a driver who would fit the classic Geordie mould of being a compulsive and livewire talker with conversational and philosophical sparks flying on the way to our first destination. It turned out that ours would have plenty to say, albeit rarely in a positive vein.

We hailed a cab and instructed our driver to take us to our bed and breakfast in Whitley Bay, a 15-minute drive. Our driver had a milky left eye, but the cataracts he suffered from were not severe enough to prevent him from making constant observations, mostly disapproving, of the parade of scantily-attired Geordie youth who were clearly in full-on party mode: "Haway, will you look at the state of them lasses? Weeerin' scarves fuur skurts, are they now?!?," he said in his almost impenetrable Geordie accent. Although I lived in London for three years, I rarely journeyed farther north than Oxford, so a Newcastle (accent on the second syllable, "noo-CASTLE"—for natives) was a jarring speech pattern to which my ear was not attuned. A great example of Geordie pronunciation—provided by Ben the previous evening in Kew Gardens—is the well-known Tyneside restaurant, Heym, which is how a Newcastle native would pronounce "home."

Dave mentioned to our cabdriver that we would be hiking the length of the Wall and asked what the weather would be like the next day. "Neeeece and sooony," he replied, "and why the hell are ya walkin', there are adders on that trail, so there are—is it a car that you need?" Dave mentioned that I was a veteran of Appalachian Trail ("AT") hikes, and the possibility of a chance encounter with a snake was not worrisome and indeed bordered upon the mundane. That set our driver off on a long monologue where I was lucky to catch one word in three. The monologue quickly evolved into a diatribe, but I did manage to decipher the subject of his ire—the larger brewing companies had swallowed up many of the local pubs that we passed on our drive. These soulless mega-brewers had in turn forced a modernization of traditional pubs that had largely severed their connections with the local communities. However, for the most part the driver might as well have been speaking in Martian, and I finally gave up on trying to follow him as we made our way into Whitley Bay.

We were staying at the Lighthouse, a bed and breakfast in the middle of a long section of terraced housing sloping downward to the seashore. Jerry, the amiable owner, also had an impenetrable and high velocity Geordie accent, and I politely nodded my head as he gave detailed instructions for every light switch, nozzle and spigot in my eccentric, nautically themed room, with lamps fashioned as lighthouses providing the cherry on top. Dave mentioned that in the tour of his room, Jerry helpfully offered that the colorful lights at a nearby fair partly visible from his window were not "aliens landing" and that it was safe for us to venture out for our dinner.

At Turknaz, the Turkish restaurant down the street, literally a few meters away from the Whitley Bay beach and the North Sea, Dave and I discussed the upcoming hike over an excellent dinner and an unrecorded number of Istanbul's "Efes" beer. We would be "slack-packing"—we had hired Sherpa Expeditions to handle our accommodations and luggage transport for our six-day journey. During our daily hikes, we would only be carrying small backpacks containing essentials such as water, snacks, and maps. Our main luggage, courtesy of Sherpa, would be awaiting us when we arrived at our destination each evening. To me, this was a luxurious arrangement compared to most of my extended hiking trips along the AT, which usually entailed carrying 30–35 pounds on my back, including a tent and sleeping bag. There would be no outdoor camping on this trip—we would be spending our evenings in small country inns and bed and breakfasts along the way. For Dave, who by his own admission had avoided camping or hiking overnight anywhere since "the distinctly uncherished experience of a school army cadet force camp in The Brecon Beacons region of western Wales." He readily acknowledged his status as a fully-fledged London "lightweight," and slack packing was therefore the only acceptable arrangement.

We left the restaurant at about 9 p.m. and strolled the short distance down to the sea wall. It was high tide, and the waves were crashing against the promenade, about thirty feet below. My nostrils were filled with a strong whiff of kelp and briny North Sea surf, an episodic memory scent I had not thought of for years but instantly recognized. Since it was evening, there was, unfortunately, no squawk of seagulls, the accompanying melody to the salty air that always brings back memories of English beaches.

I mused about family holidays to Whitley Bay in the 1960s, in a house five minutes from where we were staying that evening, when we had visits to the "Spanish City" fair (referenced by Dire Straits in their nostalgic and haunting hit song "Tunnel of Love"), and my boyhood joy in discovering an abandoned scooter half-buried in the beach.

I wished we had more time to spend in the area; the faded glory of an old English beach resort town was sure to produce many tarnished and unexpected charms. But planned hikes always force choices, and the timetable required that we finish by Friday. We walked back up the hill to Jerry's bed and breakfast quietly excited and a bit nervous over the unknown journey that loomed ahead.

* * *

Jerry greeted us in the dining area the next morning and poured us coffee. "Of all the Americans I haff met, the one who liked Doan-old Troomp the most was a Mexican lass," he volunteered. Not wanting to get dragged into a prolonged discussion of American politics before we pushed off on our hike, I nodded my head politely and changed the subject to the pending collapse of Thomas Cook. Thomas Cook was a venerable British travel company that was on the verge of bankruptcy, brought to its knees by the intense price competition offered by lower cost online travel agencies. Many vacationers, like Jerry, were worried about pending trips that had been prepaid, and whether the vacations would be honored or not. Jerry glanced nervously on the small television that was set up in the dining area to monitor updates on the latest developments.

As he delivered my breakfast of scrambled eggs, smoked salmon, British back bacon and wheat toast, Jerry briefed us on our starting point, the site of the original Roman fort named Segedunum, at Wallsend our pronunciation of which he was quick to correct as rhyming with "Pals End." Despite my continuing difficulties in tuning in to the Geordie dialect and delivery, I was already developing a vision of northeastern England locals who were open, friendly, and free with gently jabbing and lighthearted banter. I kept thinking of Andy Capp as the caricature of a Geordie. Capp was the Hartlepool based ne'er-do-well but charming working-class hero featured in Reg Smythe's mid-century comic strip.

Our pre-arranged cab picked us up at 9 a.m.; the chiseled, gimlet-eyed driver seemed to embody another caricature—that of the no-nonsense young Geordie male—"he looked so hard that he might have been born with tattoos" was Dave's droll assessment when we were safely out of the car. I had instructed him to drive us to Segedunum, which he did not comprehend, probably due to my mangled American enunciation. I sank back in my seat and let Dave handle the directions from that point forward which he successfully managed by dumbing-down the drop-off coordinates to a car park adjacent to the Asda (Walmart) grocery supermarket in Wallsend.

The Roman fort at Segedunum ("Strong Fort" in Latin) marked the official eastern extremity of Hadrian's Wall. Adjacent to its original location is now a museum shaped to resemble the helmet and facemask of a period Roman centurion. It took a while for the likeness to sink in, and Dave and I originally mistook it for an air traffic control tower. As unprepossessing as the Wallsend car park had seemed, the presence of the mask/museum overlooking and guarding the commencement of Hadrian's Wall was a cleverly conceived and eye-catching bit of architecture.

The decision to string together the 84-mile (135-kilometer) public footpath ("the Wall Path" or "Path"—except the fifteen miles leading through Newcastle, which is called "Hadrian's Way") that closely tracks the original wall was not made until 1996, and it took seven years and almost $10 million for the trail to be completed—by contrast, it only took the Romans six years to build the actual Wall. Prior to the formal Path being finalized, intrepid hikers who wished to walk along the shadow of the Wall were at the mercy of unwieldy

Segedunum Museum architecture echoing the form of the centurion sculpture standing guard nearby (David Wilmot).

maps and an almost total lack of signage. Local farmers would sometimes charge hikers for traversing their plots of land, and would even refuse access outright, forcing long and time-consuming detours. Not only did rights of way over private property need to be secured, but archaeologists had to be present for every change made along the Path—each signpost, fence and bench had to be approved in order to ensure that the original wall was not damaged in any way. While only about ten miles of the original stone wall still remain, the areas adjoining it were often used for forts, barracks, marketplaces and bathhouses, and the integrity of these remains also needed to be safeguarded.[3] There are sections of the Wall owned by the National Trust, most notably, the area around Housesteads Fort. One long stretch between Heddon-on-the Wall to Chollerford is owned by the Northumberland Highway Department. But most of the land along the hike is privately owned and stitching together permissions from hundreds of different property owners had the effect of stretching out the Path, which bobs and weaves according to the willingness of individual landowners to allow hikers to tromp across their farmland. This created inevitable detours from the site of the actual Wall and resulted in a Path that is 14 miles longer than the original Roman barrier.

Dave and I, like an estimated 60 percent of the estimated 5,000 hikers[4] who complete the entire Path each year, were walking from east to west. The main advantage for going in this direction was tackling the roughly fifteen miles of greater Newcastle at the onset. An extended urban landscape, while certainly an interesting change of pace from the wilderness hiking I was accustomed to in the United States, was also a hurried backdrop that we wanted to complete at the start. Our guidebooks assured us that the scenery gradually improved as one headed westward, in the form of farmland, upland moors, riverine dales and tidal flats—the soft and alluring northern English vistas that I had long associated with Hadrian's Wall. The main disadvantage in walking in a westerly direction was the possibility of hiking into stiff headwinds, which tend to blow in from the west in England.

The Path starts on a brick walkway and winds towards the River Tyne, the waterway that helped fuel Newcastle's glorious industrial past as the world's leading shipbuilding powerhouse—at one point, 25 percent of the world's ships were manufactured in Newcastle, and the first modern Japanese navy was built on the Tyne in the late 19th century. Prior to that, both the Union and Confederate armies during the American Civil War used artillery manufactured in Newcastle's bustling factories. "There is not its like in thirteen miles of river the world over" was a quote from 1924 emblazoned on a metal tourist sign we passed. The quote evoked a bygone era of industrial age Newcastle, when the shoreline of the River Tyne was packed with a seemingly endless stretch of crowded shipyards, smoke belching forges, trains loudly hissing steam and cavernous warehouses.

We passed chain-linked fences topped with razor wire guarding the abandoned Swan Hunter shipyard, closed since 2007, when all of the plant's equipment and machinery were sold and shipped to India.[5] Swan Hunter is perhaps best known as the shipyard where the RMS Mauretania was built in 1906. It was during the clearing for the slipway for this massive ocean liner that the only section of Wall between Newcastle and Wallsend was discovered. She was, at the time, the world's largest passenger ship and set the speed record for an ocean liner, covering the distance from Southampton to New York in just five days.[6] The musician Sting, who perhaps ranks in the top tier of the Geordie rock and roll pantheon, grew up in the shadows of the Swan Hunter shipyard and used this as inspiration for his writing of the music and lyrics for "The Last Ship," an original musical which opened in Los Angeles in January 2020, just before Covid arrived.

The early morning cloudiness had dissipated and was replaced by a gentle sunshine that nudged temperatures up into the mid–60s. We were planning on hiking to the village of Wylam, a distance of about 20 miles—certainly an ambitious undertaking for our first day, but the Path was almost entirely flat. We would be hugging the northern bank of the Tyne in greater Newcastle for the first ten miles before gradually making our way into the countryside.

The asphalt path was bordered by fences, many covered in graffiti, and the bushes, uncut grass and weeds that lined it were flecked with cityscape detritus—cigarette butts, empty cans of lager, torn packets of crisps and discarded newspapers. Some of the graffiti was of the expected sinister, post-punk anarchist variety, other bits were engaging, including the colorful script painted on a long section of a brick viaduct that ran above the mock-Tudor style Tyne Bar: "Stone holds the bird ... air and water sing the song ... steel becomes an angel's shape ... and you are all these things." These lines, I later learned, were from the renowned Newcastle children's novelist David Almond. Dave mentioned that the angel reference by either Almond or the graffiti artist was likely connected to the iconic "Angel of the North," a 66-foot-high steel sculpture

Graffiti along pathway in Newcastle (Mark Clegg).

erected in 1998 in nearby Gateshead. In another shining example of the irrepressible Geordie spirit, a massive replica jersey of Alan Shearer, the legendary Newcastle United footballer, once draped the Angel.

We chatted about the "North Country" and its stature within England. My own experience while living in the UK was very myopic and London-centric, and my perspective of the entire country was dominated by the three years I lived there. It is difficult for an American to understand the influence of London relative to the rest of the nation, because we have no similar economic, political and cultural colossus in the United States. Greater London comprises one-third of the total GDP of the United Kingdom. One would have to combine the states of California, Texas, New York and Illinois to arrive at a similar concentration of economic clout in America.

All ten of the highest circulation newspapers are based in London; the capital city is not only the center of British, but also European, banking and finance. London is the hub of British television and film production, and in a typical year, the 20-member English Premier League (soccer) includes five to six teams from the sprawling southeastern metropolis.

The northern cities of Manchester, Liverpool, Sheffield and Newcastle were a blank slate to me other than a collection of random facts (many supplied by Dave) I had assembled over the years about their rock and roll groups and professional sports teams. My less than informed impression was that they were similar to the rust belt cities in the United States like Buffalo, Cleveland, Detroit and Pittsburgh, idiosyncratic and rich in their own local culture, but also living off of faded glory with populations leaving in droves to the Sunbelt for greater economic opportunity.

This facile disregard of the "North Country" is widespread. I recently cleaned out a stack of tourist brochures and old back issues of *Realm* magazine (since renamed *Discover Britain*)—a traditional tourist-oriented publication geared to North American visitors. While thumbing through a stack of twenty or so copies, the only areas in the north that were deemed worthy of attracting the wallets of tourists were the Lake District and Yorkshire Dales. There was no mention of "Hadrian's Wall Country" or any of the mid-sized historically relevant cities like Durham and Carlisle.

Signposts displaying the white acorn, which signifies a National Trail in Britain, periodically marked the Path. These acorns, like the white rectangular slash marks on trees on the Appalachian Trail, were our beacons, assurance that we were headed in the right direction. Their worth was perhaps even more profound when navigating the post-industrial maze of Newcastle—after the Path would seemingly dead end, we would spot an acorn painted on the side of an abandoned warehouse, notifying us of an upcoming sharp turn. It was to prove during our hike that our constant adherence to the guidance offered by the white acorns served us well and we coined

The white acorn symbol (Mark Clegg).

the Latin motto *"candidum amicum glandem"*—"the white acorn is your friend"—both as a hike credo and as a homage to the ancient Roman architects of the Wall.

Hadrian's Wall ("the Wall") had long ago been dismantled in greater Newcastle—the limestone blocks were carted off for other uses, beginning in Anglo-Saxon times and continuing into the industrial era. The portions of actual Wall that still remain are almost invariably in the higher elevation areas along the Path, where the cost and exertion required in removing and hauling the stones to lower lying areas would have dwarfed any economic, military, or aesthetic benefits.

We were hiking along an area that had been created by ballast dumping (stones were used to weigh down otherwise empty wooden ships on their way to pick up cargo) from ships returning from the Thames in the 1800s before they loaded and hauled more coal from Newcastle back to London. St Anthony's Tar Works, which had shut down in 1981, still required clean up remediation to remove the toxic hydrocarbons that still floated in the River Tyne. There was graffiti covered posted signage warning us of various toxicities in case we had any bizarre thoughts about trying to make our way to the polluted shore area to fill our water bottles or take an impromptu, restorative dip. The treacly water could not be seen below the murky surface, and we watched in amazement as plastic bottles, discarded wrappers and even an inflatable sex doll drifted slowly past us towards the mouth of the river. Dave made the trenchant observation that the doll (whom we christened "The Lady of the Tyne") was returning to its home, the petrochemical ooze, from whence she came.

We made our way past the quays of Newcastle, which had been redeveloped into low-rise condominiums, gastro pubs and smart coffee shops. This is a pattern that I had seen so many times in "Rust Belt" cities of the United States—urban planners and developers, trying, with varying degrees of success, to resurrect downtrodden riverfront and downtown areas to attract the wallets of young professionals.

On this bright, sunshiny Sunday in late September, a flea market with food trucks had been set up along the riverfront. Sizzling sausages, fish and chips, and exotic blends of aromatic coffee filled the air. The riverside food markets were busy and populated with families and more fully dressed young people than those we had observed from the taxi the previous evening. Possibly some of them had been in amongst the city center revelers who had partied into the wee hours and were now in damage limitation mode, nursing their hangovers with one of the mouthwatering Cumberland Sausage-in-a-baguette lunches, which were hissing from the grills in the barbecue stalls. It was tempting to "climb-in" on these for an impromptu lunch, but we could still feel the benefit of Jerry's "slap-up" breakfast in Whitley Bay and settled for an espresso before continuing our walk. We also decided to skip an early meal and combine lunch with dinner in the late afternoon at a pub in Wylam. We had already covered almost half of the 20-mile distance in just over three hours, and we showed no signs of fatigue.

We passed the stunning succession of Newcastle's seven bridges that span the Tyne as the cityscape slowly morphed into housing estates and industrial parks. Still no greenswards or signs of a soothing, soft countryside, but we felt that we were beginning to leave the city behind us after crossing several footbridges over busy motorways.

We passed a sign to Blaydon, and Dave informed me that it was the site of the famous horse track and subject of the Geordie ditty— and adopted anthem of the Newcastle United football team—*Blaydon Races.* The song was written in the 19th century to celebrate the rollicking good times to be had at a day at the races during the Victorian era. As a hedonistic call-to-arms it has always encapsulated the good cheer, fueled by more than a few Newcastle Brown Ales, which embodied the vibrant local spirit:

> *Ah me lads, ye shudda seen us gannin',*
> *We pass'd the foaks alang the road just as they wor stannin';*
> *Thor wis lots o' lads an' lassies there, aal wi' smiling faces,*
> *Gannin' alang the Scotswood Road, to see the Blaydon Races.*[7]

The association of *Blaydon Races* to Newcastle United was typical of Dave's bottomless grasp on matters related to sports. Over the years, he has helped broaden my understanding on such serious topics as to why "Annie's Song," "You'll Never Walk Alone," "The Battle Hymn of the Republic," and "Swing Low" are used as musical accompaniment by the supporters of professional and national teams in stadiums throughout England. Perhaps most perplexingly, the Premier League (soccer) team I supported, Chelsea FC, adopted the children's nursery rhyme "One Man Went to Mow" as its unofficial anthem.

And the conclusion I have reached after years of pondering on this highly serious subject is (a) that both large and small crowds at sporting event are predisposed to communal singing (b) that they are even more likely to stick to even an unlikely choice of anthem if they are confident that everyone will remember the words. I was at Twickenham, the home of English rugby, when the strains of "Swing Low" were first heard at a major international match and to this day believe that it caught on because the crowd could still remember the words even under the extreme pressure which a day's drinking can exert upon one's memory. In contrast, many a time prior to this occasion I had heard the gathered England faithful try to sing through both verses of "Jerusalem" with it invariably breaking down in repetition or the mixing of lines from different verses—and particularly if attempted towards the end of the match. So "Swing Low" it was to be and has been ever since.

Just beyond Lemington, the ambience softened as we began to pass small family-owned farms with carefully tended vegetable gardens. The Path, lined with wild thyme, ox-eye daisies, yellow ragwort and yarrow, wound its way through an abandoned railway track and past lush, overgrown bushes that still held the last of the summer's blackberries, which we pulled and ate while walking. We passed what appeared to be a local fête, which included a dog show. One lovely old lady spoke to us about her dog, which "sang along with the hymns at the local church." Unfortunately, we never got to witness this well-meaning canine chorus, but the idea of it was truly heartwarming.

In Scotswood, we passed a statue of a poignant rendering of the 1925 Montagu View pit disaster, caused by an inrush of water from a nearby abandoned pit, which claimed 22 men and boys from that small village alone. The statue featured a coal miner leading a pit pony with two small children riding on its back. The miner's head is turned to the left, looking southward to the Scotswood Bridge that spans the Tyne. The motif is one of hope, memorializing the past while looking forward to the future (the girl is snapping a picture of the miner with her cellphone).

I found the statue oddly moving. The miner reminded me of the time in my youth when we lived in the north of England, when industrial disputes in the mining industry were frequent and very bitter. Whilst we did not live in an industrialized area, such disputes when they happened would frequently dominate conversation and occasionally family life when coal shortages resulted in planned power cuts. On those evenings in the early 1970s we would play a pictorial game of "beetles" by candlelight, which I suspect was something my parents had done in their youth as well. Through my readings of, for example, George Orwell's "The Road to Wigan Pier," the historic plight of the miners was something I was very aware of, and quite frankly fascinated by. This, alongside the considerable quantity of war films and documentaries, which were broadcast on television at the time, made UK society sometimes feel overly nostalgic and backward looking. We were somehow unable and unwilling to fully detach ourselves from the turbulent events that my parents and their generation had lived through. In contrast, what I loved about the statue was the child enthusiastically holding the smartphone and cherishing nothing but the present day and an absorption in the delights and possibilities offered by modern technology. I would be the first to argue that we have so much to learn from our history, and I advocate the importance of remembrance of past sacrifices, but the statue made me think of my three children and how contemporary tech has contributed to cementing their thinking, interests and outlook much more into present day culture than was the case in my youth. None of which I regret, by the

---

way, but I have to admit to affectionately thinking of their adhesive relationships with their smart phones and their look-forward mentality upon surveying the statue.

I mentioned to Mark that the hard-nosed working-class pride that represented the northeast region of England generated a cool factor in 1970s Britain, when coal miners were still numerous and emblematic of a proud northern heritage. This was before the massive pit closures in the 1980s followed by strikes and violent standoffs with the government of Prime Minister Margaret Thatcher.

The statue also reminded me of "Jarrow Song," written by Newcastle native and former Animals member Alan Price, who penned the lyrics in 1974 in commemoration of unemployed Geordie shipyard workers who marched on the House of Commons in 1936. This was perhaps the best known of the "Hunger Marches" from the 1920s and 1930s that highlighted the dire conditions of the working class in Britain in the interwar period.

The plight of the mineworkers was captured by the paintings of the Ashington Group, a small society of artists from Ashington, Northumbria, established in 1934. The group was composed largely of miners from the Northumbrian Woodhorn and Ellington Collieries and who, despite no formal artistic training, were encouraged by their tutor, Robert Lyon to create their own paintings based upon their experiences. They grew in notoriety, were exhibited in London, and prominent collectors such as Helen Sutherland acquired some items of their work. Oliver Kilbourn, one of the group's leading members, put the paintings into trust and today they are on permanent show at the Woodhorn Colliery Museum in Ashington.[8] The activities of the Ashington Group were captured in William Feaver's book "The Pitmen Painters" that was also turned into a stage play,[9] which was performed at the National Theatre.

At about the fifteen-mile mark, my legs and feet were becoming noticeably sore. This soreness stayed with me for the entire trip and persisted for months after I returned to America, particularly in the area behind my kneecaps. We had walked on almost nothing except

Statue of Montagu Pit Disaster (David Wilmot).

asphalt throughout the day, and this pounding of the pavement had acted as a meat tenderizer by putting enormous pressure on the back of my legs and the bottom of my feet. I had packed a pair of running shoes for the hike; my heavy duty, over the ankle mountain boots were deemed too heavy to bring along for a hike that featured little in the way of the rugged mountain hiking that I was accustomed to in the eastern United States.

Cornfields, rugby pitches and even a golf course bordered the last five miles on the approach to Wylam, which was three miles off of the official Path. Lack of lodging options along this section of the hike forced us to take this detour, and we would of course be forced to retrace the exact same three miles the next morning before we could resume our journey on the Path. The main danger along this stretch was dodging the bicyclists who zoomed past us, at close range and unannounced.

This section was formerly part of the Wylam Waggonway, which originally used horse-drawn wagons and later steam locomotives to transport coal from the nearby collieries to Newcastle and the River Tyne. Along the way, we passed the cottage of George Stephenson, who is known as "the Father of Railways," and formed the first publicly held railway.[10]

Wylam's major influence upon the development of the railways is emphasized by the "Puffing Billy," the world's oldest surviving steam locomotive. The locomotive was constructed in 1813–14 for Christopher Blackett, the owner of Wylam Colliery as a means of replacing horses as the source of motive power on the tramway. The train is believed to have been a major influence upon George Stephenson and the adoption of steam locomotives by other collieries in the North East of England. The name "Puffing Billy" continues to be commonly recognized and used in England.

At the centre of Wylam village we passed by a nine-meter-high hexagonal, Gothic-style cenotaph memorial commemorating the town's soldiers who fell during both the Great War and the Second World War. Its three plaques listed 53 names in total and one can only imagine and shudder at the thought of the devastation that must have been felt by Wylam's community.[11] The 1911 Census[12] of Wylam Civil Parish listed 295 homes and 1,312 inhabitants, including 610 males. Some 42 of the soldiers listed on the memorial were Great War casualties and the remains of many were never repatriated. This colossal loss of life for such a small village is highlighted by an unattributed quote on Wylam's page in the North East War Memorial Project website that "an average of one in every six of our little community had offered themselves for the defence of our liberties."[13] *Situated as it is close to the Hadrian's Wall Path, the memorial is a stark reminder that nearly two millennia since Hadrian's time, the risk of terrible conflict arising from a complacent attitude to the growth of nationalism and extremism continues to lurk in the background.*

One of Wylam's sons is not listed on the memorial but did tragically die shortly after the Great War and has a remarkable story. Captain Frederick George "Dusty" Dunn was born in Wylam and was awarded the Air Force Cross for valor.[14] *His personal background as the son of a Wylam miner was completely at odds with the perhaps clichéd image of the Royal Flying Corps ("RFC") being filled with privileged members of the "ruling class." His parents moved to London in 1908 when Dusty was 14 to work as domestic servants for a wealthy family. Upon the outbreak of the War in July 1914, Dusty, at the age of 19, volunteered for immediate active service despite only having 40 hours of solo flying experience. Considering the often-quoted average life expectancy of three weeks for RFC pilots during the War, his survival throughout the hostilities was remarkable, surviving multiple missions and two crashes. He completed his war service as a flight commander, and was appointed chief pilot of the Tarrant Tabor, a huge British triplane which had been intended for wartime use but in the aftermath of World War I was in the process of being adapted for civilian use and was also being considered as the prototype of the first plane to attempt a trans–Atlantic flight. On the morning of Monday May 26, 1919, in front of invited journalists, Dusty managed to get the plane airborne but almost immediately it nose-dived and crashed, killing both him and his co-pilot.*

We made our way into town at 3:30, and our requests for food were declined at the first two pubs we entered—both establishments had "run out." It was noticeable that both pubs were very full and brimming with adults and youngsters having an extended Sunday lunch. Given that Wylam is a small village, it struck us that these pubs appeared to be a centerpiece of local community life and the opposite of the taverns of Newcastle which yesterday's cab driver had fairly or unfairly maligned as corporate and stale. I managed a peek back into the kitchen in one pub and saw heaping amounts of roast beef and Yorkshire pudding, so it was less likely a lack of food but a staff that wanted to go home early that prevented us from satiating our ravenous appetites.

Completely famished, we made our way to the last possible choice, the Fox and Hounds ("Fooks 'n' Hoonds"), which happened to be directly across the street from our lodging for the evening in the center of town, the Wormald House. Although it was just past their cut-off time for meals (at a little past 4 p.m.), they agreed to serve us. It was probably not the freshest meal which the pub had served on that Sunday, but a steaming plate of sliced pork, roasted potatoes, broccoli, carrots and green peas—simple, unadorned English fare that was disappointing only in the sense that it did not feature the third root vegetable staple, parsnips. The arrival of a pint of bitter further restored my spirits. The IPA craze in the United States had slowly made its way to the UK, and most of the taps at the bar featured different brands of that over-hopped monstrosity. But I was relieved to find a lone traditional English bitter out of the numerous selections on tap.

We left the Fox and Hounds in good moods having made impressively short work of their last Sunday Roast serving of the day. So hungry had I been that I regarded our server as having gained "Good Samaritan" status given the limited possibility of eating as well anywhere else that evening. As we were leaving the pub we experienced another example of North Country bonhomie when a pub-goer who slipped outside for a cigarette noticed our hiking apparel and spoke to us. Wearing a black leather jacket and a t-shirt sporting the name of the glam rock band Kiss, he looked more suited to a darkened and ear-splitting music pub in downtown Newcastle. While puffing on his cigarette and smoothing back his black, slicked-back hair, he spoke

*animatedly about the health benefits of hiking and was very knowl-
edgeable about the walking routes in the local area. He also spoke
very favorably about the landlord of our next place of stay, having known his family for a long time. This openness and even eager-
ness to assist a complete stranger was typical of the North East
and quite different to what one would typically experience in London where such outward demonstrations of helpfulness are more
sporadic.*

We walked across the street to Wormald House where we met
David, the effusive owner. He had, as a courtesy, already booked us at
a nearby pizza restaurant, thinking we would not have many options
for dining on a Sunday evening. We thanked him for his thoughtful-
ness, and told him that that was not necessary; we had just stuffed
ourselves royally at the nearby pub.

It had been years since I had stayed at a British B&B, and I had
forgotten the personalized walk-thru tour owners typically provide.
I was beginning to remember that each room was unique in its own
way in terms of lighting and plumbing, and I was never sure, even
after a detailed explanation, of how to turn anything on. I was especially wary of anything with a string attached; I knew if I pulled it the
slightest bit too hard, it would come out of its fixture—my natural
tendency for years was to try and force things until they ultimately
broke; now I overcompensate and just give up if something doesn't
work immediately. I will sit in the dark or do without hot water if the
alternative is to sheepishly ask again for instructions or risk pulling
a cord out of the wall. The keys were also the large, jailer style ver-
sions on a metal ring, just about impossible to lose but requiring just
the right amount of positioning in the keyhole and a skillful jiggle to
open a door.

Dave and I left the B&B after dusk and made our way down the
hill and over the bridge, which spanned the churning Tyne. We found
the Boathouse Pub, opposite the tiny two platform train station that
was built in 1835 with an ancient red stationmaster's box suspended
by a metal truss over the rail line. All of this is captured in a quite

Watercolor of the Boathouse Pub at Wormald House in Wylam (David Wilmot).

splendid watercolor painting, which David had hung on the wall in the hallway of Wormald House.

Dave and I found a table close to the bar and placed our orders. I decided to branch out and asked for an artisanal gin—small, boutique distillers of gin had sprung up all over England and Scotland, and they were quite the rage in 2019. I randomly selected one, and then had to choose a mixer—there had likewise been an explosion in choices for tonic water (many under the umbrella uber-brand of Fever Tree), and after scanning the selections for about thirty seconds, I finally picked the one with the most eye-catching label.

Whilst ordering a Peroni "heart-starter" (my usual appellation for the first drink of the evening after a hard day's hiking), I casually observed that the gentrification of the traditional utilitarian "G and T" drink had reached the point in the UK where the appropriate tonic mixer now seemed to be as important as the brand of gin itself. Fever Tree tonic mixers had become massively popular within a matter of a few years and alongside the multiplicity of artisanal gins that have become available; the combination has unquestionably taken on a new lease on life as a drink "to be seen with."

We settled in with our drinks and soaked in the scene. It was more crowded than what I would have expected for a Sunday night, and even more surprisingly, it was packed with locals. My experience with English pubs, certainly in London and in the traditional Cotswold and West Country tourist haunts, was based on a healthy mixture or even a preponderance of outsiders vs. locals. It was not at all unusual, for instance, to find more foreigners than British in the popular South Kensington and Chelsea pubs in London that I used to frequent.

It struck me, as I listened to their conversations, that I was well off the beaten tourist track. Posters on the pub wall announcing upcoming music nights and darts leagues hinted at the ongoing social life of the village, which continued throughout the year. Certainly, thousands of people hike Hadrian's Wall each year, but we were on the tail end of the peak-hiking season. Reduced daylight, cooler temperatures and heavier rain bring with them a reduction in hiking traffic in September that does not begin to pick up again until spring—many bed and breakfasts that rely on hikers shut down in October. The isolated hamlets and villages that we would be visiting in Northumberland and Cumbria were, like the trail towns I passed through on the Appalachian Trail, heavily reliant on hikers to provide a hefty portion of their annual tourist related revenues.

The conversations that we overheard ranged from local gossip to the previous evening's disappointing performance by Newcastle United to the upgrade in clientele over the years at the Fox and Hounds pub. The northern burr was becoming a bit more decipherable, and I was able to make out that that the "Fooks n' Hoonds," where we had enjoyed our late lunch, was formerly "packed with nowt but lasses who were all fur coats and nae knickaz [panties]."

That was an eyebrow raising observation to be making, even more so in public, but in fairness to the old-timer who made it, I am sure that he was oblivious to his own unfashionable caveman rhetoric.

When I lived in London I never traveled to the countryside without my thick, dog-eared copy of The *Good Pub Guide*, the two-inch thick and extraordinarily detailed bible for pub aficionados. I would highlight each pub I visited, with notes written in the margin. I immediately wondered if the quirky Boathouse merited a mention in my now ancient version of the Guide (when I got back home, I was pleased to discover that it merited a short, favorable recommendation in the 1993 edition). Dave later informed me that the updated 2020 version awarded a "3" rating, which I thought was a cruel injustice, even when adjusting for the lofty standards maintained by *The Good Pub Guide.*

Like many of my perceptions of England, my view of traditional pubs was locked in a late 1980s–early 1990s time warp before they became, in the words of Paul Kingsnorth, in his book, *Real England: The Battle Against the Bland*, "gastro'd or corporatized. [An English pub] was an unremarkable little place, which is why we liked it. The landlord has two enormous old English bulldogs that look like they want to eat you but actually want to be scratched under the chin. A gang of old boys gathers for darts tournaments every week, to play, to smoke too much, and cackle at private jokes. The walls are hung by badly stuffed fish. There are armchairs and an open fire."[15]

Smoking, of course, is now strictly prohibited in pubs (a good thing), but the musty and genuine ambience has left with it, leaving many pubs with a polished chrome and potted plant contrived atmosphere. The threadbare carpet and the creaking floors with cask ale taps requiring more muscle to pull than galley oars have largely disappeared.

Pubs have been closing by the hundreds in the English countryside over the previous decades. Overall, more than 25 percent of pubs in the UK have shut down just since the start of the Millennium.[16] Villages have been hit particularly hard: It has been estimated that over half of villages in England are now "publess."[17] The two main reasons for this decline have been a fall off in the popularity of beer—overall beer sales have plummeted by one-third since 1980—coupled with consumers choosing lower cost alternatives for their purchases, such as grocery stores and other retailers. Less than half of all beer consumed now in the UK is in pubs, versus 88 percent in 1980.[18] Dave offered up another reason drawn from personal experience as his children progressed from high school to university. The cost of drinking in pubs has become prohibitively high for students to spend their entire evenings in one, and this economic truth gave birth to the concept of the "pre-lash" or "pre-drinks" (consisting of more drinks—for example, a liter bottle of cheap supermarket vodka) before venturing out and buying only one or two drinks on the town. The same phenomenon was occurring in the United States—my young adult children referred to it as "pre-gaming."

In light of this depressing set of facts, it was thrilling to find a throwback pub such as the Boathouse that was clearly a communal gathering point in a small town largely shielded from the onslaught of tourists. I have no idea if a large brewing company owned the pub, if it had contract arrangements with large brewers or if in fact the array of ales on tap were former micro-ales that had been bought out by the global brewing behemoths. Certainly it had some standing for the quality of its ales with no less than 15 CAMRA (Campaign for Real Ale) awards gracing one of its walls. Whatever the truth was about its ownership and contracts, for a couple of hours on a Sunday evening, life stood still, unbothered by the gathering storm of a new week with its newly emerging disheartening news cycles just hours away.

Dave and I discussed Brexit, a topic that would be frequently visited over the course of our hike. At that time, the British Prime Minister, Boris Johnson, had suspended Parliament in an arcane maneuver referred to as "proroguing." A break with the European was scheduled to occur by October 31.

Dave is a successful owner in a London based private investment firm, and our career paths diverged after the Great Recession, which left him and his previous business relatively unscathed, while mine in the United States and its dependence on the real estate sector, was left devastated. I had never quite figured out Dave's exact political leanings—my best guess was that he was a "wet" pro–Europe Tory or perhaps an occasional supporter of the Liberal Democrats.

In this regard I can understand Mark's uncertainty as to my political stance. The left-wing leanings of my early teens dissipated as I studied Government and Politics at school and became less enamored with a fixed alignment with any political party and more focused upon a small number of issues such as electoral reform and proportional representation. My beliefs were not in any way a rejection of the outcome of the UK's EU referendum vote—quite the opposite—democracy is the foundation stone of UK society and the country had made its decision. So I am not critical of the decision to exit or the actions of politicians in trying to implement the transition to non-membership of the EU. My disappointment with the exit process that was playing out in front of us reflected my personal dismay, having spent most of my adult life working within a European context and relishing feeling part of such a diverse and multi-faceted continent. That pro–European mindset had been handed down to me at a relatively early age and had been reinforced over the years by my own experiences.

In the run-up to the 2016 Referendum, much of the campaigning of the Leave lobby focused upon economic arguments, whereas my take on it focused on the desire to remain in partnership with Europe. This emanates from opinions formed in my youth and conversations that I held then with elder members of my family. One in particular is embossed upon my memory and in a recent conversation with my mother, she recalled it almost word for word. In my grandmother's bungalow in Exeter, Devon, in the early 1970s, we were discussing the prospect of the first national referendum to determine whether the UK should remain part of the then European Economic Community ("EEC"). My recollection of the prevailing zeitgeist at the time was that we were approaching the EEC as an issue from a mixed perspective consisting of ideological optimism and amused curiosity. The UK still felt like the home of the "island race" and it was quite unusual to travel overseas, despite the proximity of Continental Europe. Calais, for example, in Northern France is a third of the distance from London as the capital is from Edinburgh but in the early 1970s a visit to Scotland on holiday would generally be more likely than a trip across the English Channel by sea or air. So there was an element of fun and fascination at the thought of having to embrace the concept of being part of a European partnership and speculating upon what it would all mean. In those far more innocent days, we used to listen to a humorous West Country singer called Adge Cutler. Adge would dress up and perform on stage in farmyard clothing to a devoted local following. His barnstorming "Drink Up Thy Cider" was his crowd-pleasing epic and was often referred to as the "National Anthem of North Somerset and Bristol." It is still sung to this day by the supporters of Bristol City Football Club during matches as a paean to West Country hedonism. As a misery-diversion strategy, I even managed to teach the ditty to my Northern school friends on that depressing long coach ride home from Yorkshire the day I lost my glasses up high on the Ingleborough Fells. Adge also penned the joke song "When the Common Market Comes to Stanton Drew"—the Common Market being another name often used for the EEC. It was the closest—which is to say not very close at all—to political commentary that the jovial Adge and his "farmyard favourites" repertoire ever came. Nonetheless, lines in the song such as "they'll say ou la la, oui oui, instead of how is thee?" and "we'll watch them foreign blokes with great big hats and cloaks, flamenco-ing down on the village green" were warm, simple and funny and of their time but strangely highlighted the fact that relatively few of us had very much first-hand experience about the diverse nations and cultures of continental Europe.

But the idea of a united Europe was the weightier issue under consideration that day in Exeter, which brings me back to that conversation in my grandmother's house. Present in addition to my grandmother was her eldest son—my uncle—a wonderful, clever man with a fantastic smile, and my parents. He was one of three brothers, each of whom fought, in his case with the Eighth Army in North Africa, through the entirety of the Second World War and returned to my relieved and thankful grandmother and mother ready, no doubt, to live a little and to try to reclaim some of their lost years. My mother recounted stories of the boys holding endless rowdy parties at their house and being kept awake by choruses of the Labour Party anthem "The Red Flag." She told me that this was not as a sign of any political affiliation but rather reflected the feeling that they wanted to take control of their lives and move away from taking orders from the officer class. This desire of their generation to put as much distance as they could between their new lives and their wartime existence was quite widespread in the UK and was a key contributor to the Conservative Party's defeat under Winston Churchill in the 1945 General Election, losing to Clement Attlee's Labour Party.

My uncle, for his part, clearly got on with rebooting his life very quickly as he joined Exeter City Football Club (nicknamed "the Grecians") and scored two goals in his debut match in December 1946, a 3–2 victory over Bristol Rovers. His photograph and megawatt smile, and those of his son, adorn the "Grecians Archive" website to this day. He also pushed forward and established a successful haulage business with his brothers in the West Country.

As a young lad, listening to their conversation with my parents I was captivated, I felt that they had all been around since the dawn of time and had seen and done everything and knew all that there was worth knowing about human behavior and how we should aspire to live. As they discussed the privations that they had endured in their youth and through the wartime years, and the horrors that they had seen; they did not dwell upon attributing blame but rather asserted their conviction that the future had to be about greater togetherness with other nations. In their view if there was an opportunity to achieve this through governmental alliances such as the EEC, then we should grasp it with both hands. They dismissed the economic counter arguments that membership of the EEC might cause inflation stating that

---

they would happily "pay £1 or considerably more for a pound of but-
ter" if it meant that we could be part of a European partnership (the
price of a pound of butter at the time was approximately 10 p). This
conversation provided the spark for the development of my personal
view as to the importance of a united Europe. "Brexit" was proving to
be a bitter pill to swallow, particularly thinking back to that conversa-
tion with the family elders for whom I had the utmost respect.

A couple of years ago I saw former Prime Minister David Cam-
eron with his family walking on a Cornish beach after an afternoon's
surfing. As I looked across at him, I wondered if he ever had moments
of reflection that he could have taken a different route to originally
promising the referendum on EU membership, and whether its out-
come had indeed done anything materially to heal the rifts that he
appeared to think had made its enactment inevitable in the first
place. Ultimately, as an island we will do as we always do which is
to "keep calm and carry on." I just hope that, in the wake of Brexit,
that this happens as the nation in full with all of its component parts
remaining as part of the United Kingdom.

It was salutary to think that by the time Mark and I sat down for
an evening's refreshment in Wylam that 1186 days had elapsed since
the day of the EU referendum and the UK electorate's "Leave" deci-
sion, a tortuous period which had commenced prior to the Rio Olym-
pic Games and seemed likely to stretch at least all the way to the then
scheduled timing of the Tokyo Olympiad. The EU exit negotiations
had assumed truly Kafkaesque proportions—yes, the UK electorate
had made its decision but any political consensus over a means to exit
seemed as remote as ever. The process had already seen two Conser-
vative prime ministers in David Cameron and Theresa May leaving
office, and now Boris Johnson was the latest to attempt to unblock the
constitutional stagnation, in his case through the enlistment of some
little-known parliamentary measures. I explained to Mark the live
example of this whereby the prime minister had advised Queen Eliz-
abeth II to prorogue, or suspend, Parliament, a political move seen
by many opposition politicians and commentators as an attempt to

prevent parliamentary scrutiny of HM Government's plans to leave the EU as the planned exit date of 31 October 2019 approached. The proroguing had been challenged in the courts and an appeal was due to be heard by the Supreme Court of the United Kingdom the following day. Another measure that had been thrown into this particular political potpourri was the inclusion of various so-called "Henry VIII powers" in various iterations of the EU Withdrawal Bill that would proffer government ministers with significant latitude to implement regulations to modify earlier legislation or the Withdrawal Bill itself. The fact that these measures had never been resorted to in contemporary UK politics reflected the Government's determination to "Get Brexit Done." It also depressingly amplified the complexity of the process, and widespread public exasperation on both sides of the Leave/ Remain divide as to the lack of any clear route to its resolution and the often-opaque political process. Unlike some I didn't even hold a negative view of the main players on the political stage. The most tortuous and dispiriting aspect of the long march to the exit door of the EU was not so much the actions of any specific Member of Parliament as the inevitability of a glacially slow exit progress. Once the question "leave or remain" had been posed to the UK electorate in the 2016 referendum and the answer duly received, the binary simplicity of the question did not reflect the complexity of agreeing on a format for a satisfactory departure from the EU. So the political machinery effectively dictated the process as we lurched from one inconsequential vote in the House of Commons to another without seemingly getting any closer to a definitive conclusion. There appeared to be no practical means of avoiding a protracted, morale-sapping and directionless go-slow beneath the immovable raincloud of Brexit. Having attempted to impart a suitable précis of this to Mark over beers I reflected that there were times when Franz Kafka would surely have tipped his hat in admiration at the procedural convolutions and cul-de-sacs which from a distance seemed to be playing out within the impenetrably opaque corridors of power.

We had exchanged a couple of commiserating emails in the

summer of 2016 when the Brexit referendum was passed by a margin of 52–48 percent. The outcome to the simple question posed by the referendum was binary, like coming up on red or black in a casino. My other source of irritation is that the three-letter suffix "xit" has duly entered the modern lexicon to reference any major personal or organizational exit process, in the same way that "gate" has been attached to any major scandal or controversy following the Watergate scandal in the early 1970s. Thus the departure of the Duke and Duchess of Sussex to the U.S. prompted the media creation of the controversial "Megxit" portmanteau. In the same way "Scoxit" and "Sexit" have both been suggested in the press as possible expressions to mark any future renewed drive by Scotland to leave the UK. "Mexit" could put a name on the unthinkable moment for Barcelona football fans when Lionel Messi eventually chooses his moment to either leave the great club or retire. Aggrieved as I am by the entire EU exit situation, it seems doubly unreasonable that the "xit" add-on will in the future be applied to any number of departure stories just to remind me of how we contrived to take this political fork in the road.

The EU referendum result, like the presidential election that would occur months later in the United States, shook our faith and confidence in the open and borderless international system that had allowed us to travel, conduct business and even live abroad with ease. Equally it was jolting to reflect, as we did, that the philosophical and emotional connections that we felt with other countries seemed so out of step with the insular and even xenophobic Zeitgeist. We had both fallen victims to the "bias of normalcy"—the world that we had grown up with seemed the same on the surface, and this had lulled us into a false sense of complacency. In retrospect, the signs had all been there, even if they were not obvious. The simmering rage in the body politic that brought us the events of 2016 had left us stunned and unprepared. We were still trying to cope with this tectonic populist shift towards pessimism and anger.

I expressed amazement to Dave that with Brexit just around the corner, there was no sense of impending doom. I suspected that it was just the traditional "keep calm and carry on" attitude of the British. Dave acknowledged that as a factor but offered that people on both sides of the argument were simply exhausted by the Brexit debate and had lost the energy to engage in the day-to-day drama with all its twists and turns. Tortuous procedural meanderings were regularly occurring in the House of Commons as a "hung" Parliament was stalemated, and as such, devoted a huge amount of time and effort to endless political bloviating. In this sense, it was very similar to the Trump Exhaustion Syndrome that many others and I experience in the United States. Keeping up with the daily threatening tweets and scary silliness was grueling, and I, like millions of others, cocooned myself in the normal routines of life as a coping mechanism.

The two counties we were hiking through, Northumberland and Cumbria, had voted for Brexit by a wide margin. Ironically, it has been estimated that Cumbria might be hurt more than any English county by withdrawal from the EU—the northern counties are more dependent on trade with European countries than those in the south. It is estimated that GDP in Cumbria might decline by as much as 13.2 percent as a result of Brexit.[19] Much like voting patterns in the 2016 elections in the United States, voters in rural areas voted, in many cases, against their economic self-interest when they felt their cultural identities were under assault. It reminded me of a former coal miner from Kentucky who was interviewed on television; the man, who required an oxygen tank to breathe, admitted that he would not be able to afford the expensive care required for his black lung disease had it not been for the Affordable Care Act (ACA) put in place by the Obama administration. He acknowledged that Trump wanted to eliminate ACA and leave him unable to pay his hospital and drug bills. Nonetheless, he supported Trump—giving a metaphorical finger to the elites who looked down on him was more important than his own life, if I connected the dots correctly.

I did not dare try to engage other patrons of the pub on their thoughts on Brexit. Years of living in the UK had taught me that it was "not on" to probe strangers, or even casual friends, on topics as divisive as politics and religion.

When we left the pub and headed back to our B&B, a light mist was falling as we crossed the bridge to the gentle trickling sound of the river flowing below us, and we climbed up the hill at the dawdling pace our aching legs demanded. Knowing that it was highly unlikely that I would ever pass this way again, I felt very fortunate to have discovered this largely undiscovered and timeless corner of England.

As we crossed the pedestrian footbridge over the Tyne, we looked westwards across Wylam Weir and a bend in the River Tyne towards the Wylam Railway Bridge, about a half-mile distant. This wrought iron bridge, constructed in 1876, was the first arch-rib design bridge built to support a suspended railway track. Whilst now 'in retirement' as a pedestrian footbridge spanning the river rushing underneath, it was a ground-breaking design in the late 19th century and provided yet another example of the North East of England's reputation during the Industrial Revolution as the centre of engineering innovation and excellence. As an early single span construction, it provided the prototype for the later development of both the Tyne Bridge in Newcastle (1928) and the Sydney Harbour Bridge (1932), both arched single-span bridges, which closely resemble the Wylam Railway Bridge in appearance. Indeed, reports exist of an attack on the Wylam Bridge during World War II by an off-course German Heinkel He 111 bomber. The Luftwaffe pilot was seeking the much more strategically important Tyne Bridge, located 15 miles away in Newcastle. The Wylam Railway Bridge was fortunately spared aerial destruction, with the Heinkel's bombs reportedly falling harmlessly between the neighboring villages of West Wylam and Crawcrook.[20] Once again, the vicissitudes of global warfare had been visited upon the quiet, attractive and unassuming hamlet of Wylam, and once again it had withstood them.

CHAPTER 2

The Red Lion

Monday was the Autumnal Equinox, and I looked out my window to see a light rain falling as Wylam slowly ushered in a new week. I knocked on Dave's door—I was once again befuddled by gadgetry and needed instructions on how to operate my shower. After showering, I went downstairs and met him for breakfast, where he was already seated and contemplating his various calorie packing "fry-up" options

After retiring to bed feeling "in pieces" after the first day's walk, I soon felt restored and encouraged and feeling positive about day two of our hike. Waking after a deep sleep in a strange bed I was momentarily unaware of my surroundings. Looking out of my window it reminded me of the opening scene of The Prisoner *TV series which I had idolized in the late 1960s. Filmed in the Italianate village of Portmeirion in North Wales, the drama followed the generally unsuccessful attempts of ex-spy "Number Six," played by Patrick McGoohan, to escape from the "Village." The opening scene of the first episode has the drugged Number Six waking up and groggily looking out in shocked realization at The Village. This iconic scene came to my mind as I blearily looked out at early-morning Wylam from my window, remembered the voyage into the unknown which I had embarked upon, and captured the view on my smartphone in homage to the masterpiece that was* The Prisoner.

Dave ordered the "full English breakfast," consisting of smoked haddock, scrambled eggs, back bacon (what we loosely refer to as "Canadian bacon" in the United States), mushrooms, baked beans, toast, and a stewed tomato. I have never been enamored of this array

Dave's "Number Six moment" at Wylam (David Wilmot).

of food choices for my morning meal—in my mind, baked beans are only paired with barbecued meat; mushrooms are an accompaniment to lunch or dinner, and I don't want to be in the same zip code as a stewed tomato. I chose eggs, toast, fruit and some bacon.

A side benefit of our calorie-burning lengthy daily hikes was that I felt perfectly justified in "hoovering" a monster breakfast each morning. Breakfast became something of an art form during the week with the splendid hostelries we stayed at providing the opportunity to climb into the traditional full English or poached haddock with a full range of high calorie accompaniments, safe in the knowledge that we would burn off our morning intake and more over the course of the day. Whilst we ate, we struck up conversation with a retired Canadian couple at an adjacent table that was also hiking the Path. They had recently completed the El Camino de Santiago in Spain and now, like us, were walking westward on the Path. Upon learning that this was my first hike of any significance, they were adamant that by the end I would want to repeat the experience. I confidently demurred, stating that survival rather than recreational enjoyment was my driving force and likely to remain the only game in town for me for the remainder of the week.

David (the B&B owner) was a very warm and informative host, providing tips not only about Wylam, but also our destination for that evening, Newbrough. He recommended that we take a detour which would reconnect us to the Path much more quickly than our plan to retrace the previous day's last three miles, but we politely declined. We were purists ("Candidum amicum glandem!") and short cuts were simply not on the table.

We stopped to pick up some food at the local grocer—we had read that for the next 40–50 miles, opportunities to pick up food and supplies were very limited (they turned out to be virtually non-existent). Dave, on the recommendation of his gym coach, loaded up on protein bars while I augmented my supply of chocolate energy bars and gummy fruit snacks.

I later regretted not attributing more importance to the visit to the co-op grocery shop as our last supply post before reaching Carlisle. If I had adopted the "go big or go home" nutrition intake strategy deployed at every breakfast during that week it would have helped no end in the days to come. We sallied forth from Wylam with a combination of optimism in our hearts but inadequate hiking rations—not a foolproof recipe for a wholly comfortable few days ahead of us and particularly in view of the imminent nose-dive in the quality of the weather conditions.

We had to retrace our steps for three miles that morning, the distance that covered the turnoff from the Path when we continued on to Wylam the previous afternoon. The sun had peeked out through the mist, and we were luckily going to enjoy a second day of splendid weather.

The Path that morning was filled with early morning walkers, usually accompanied by their leashed dogs. Terns shrieked overhead, a reminder that we were still only a short distance from the ocean. Owls still up, hours after dawn, hooted to each other across the ripened cornfields.

Dave remained some distance back, dialed in to his Monday morning conference call with colleagues in London, Paris, Munich and Luxembourg. He said that he was pleased to be joining the call from the "Northumberland office" and looked forward to establishing the "Cumbrian office" later in the week once we had crossed the line between the two counties on our hike. *Hike your own hike*, I had mentioned to him, and if he meant to spend a good portion of his time on the trail trying to coax deals past the finish line, so be it.

We found the turnoff back to the Path, which took us past dew-flecked rugby fields before skirting a golf course. We finally encountered our first moderate uphill segment, a climb of about 300 feet to Heddon-on-the-Wall, a former coal-mining town that is also infamously known as the point of origination of the deadly 2001 outbreak of foot and mouth disease in England. Over six million cattle and sheep across the country were put to death to finally stem the outbreak, and its cost to the British economy was an estimated three to five billion British pounds in lost agricultural and tourism income.[1]

The name "Heddon-on-the Wall" dates back to 1175 when it is attested in the Pipe Rolls[2] (ancient financial records maintained by the English Exchequer or Treasury) as Hedun. The Old English version of the name translates as "heathy hill."[3] By the time we had finished our climb to the village my legs certainly knew all about the hill and I eagerly consulted our gradient chart for the remainder of the day's hike to reassure myself that the bulk of our journey would thereafter be flat, albeit long. I was still adjusting to the thought of traversing the entirety of England on foot and was keen to periodically convince myself that I had the measure of it.

We met a Methodist minister wearing a clerical collar (colloquially referred to in the UK as a "dog collar"), who walked with us for about a quarter mile and told us a bit about the town's history before directing us to an extended portion of the Wall, on the edge of town and a short walk from the Path. I had been raised Methodist, and I noticed that Methodist Church chapels, which were typically more modest than their Church of England counterparts, seemed to be much more prevalent in the towns of northern England compared to the south. John Wesley, an 18th-century reformer of the Anglican Church that evolved into the evangelistic movement known as Methodism, started his ministry in colonial Savannah in my native state of Georgia before returning to England. He traveled extensively in the north of England, preaching and evangelizing and received one particularly rude reception in Newcastle in 1743. But rather than admonishing the unruly mob for its rude behavior, he paid them a back handed compliment by wryly observing, "They scarcely threw anything at all."[4]

Before heading back to his chapel, the helpful cleric also encouraged us to visit the magnificent Victrix life-size model of a Roman soldier wielding a chainsaw, which had been carved out of a diseased tree and now stands proudly outside Heddon's Dingle Dell café. Since we were running behind schedule, we had to skip an impromptu visit to the Dingle Dell and continued our walk through Heddon.

After our meeting with the friendly Kiss fan in Wylam the previous day and the Methodist Minister in Heddon, it was apparent both that we clearly stood out as through-hikers and that the locals were generally very friendly and eager to offer help. We would not have had the same attention walking through a larger town, but I was pleased that people would come up to talk to us, not least because we were struggling to find the main attraction in Heddon.

The sign marking the Wall was a small, unobtrusive arrow marker on the side of a wall bordering an alley that we could have easily missed if we had not been looking for it. This 700-foot stretch, running parallel to farmland, represented the widest stretch of original Wall still remaining. The Romans had originally chosen almost 10 feet width for the Wall but shortened the gauge to about 8 feet when the broader width proved too expensive and impractical for the higher, more remote regions. Until the late 19th century, a hedge had covered this section, and it wasn't fully uncovered until 1938.[5] It is estimated that about half of the Wall that is now visible was covered by turf and soil until the 20th century.

Even in its relatively unprotected state, the Wall in Heddon was well short of eye-level, only one-third of its original height of 15 feet. The stones used to build the Wall consisted of (usually) limestone facing stones on the front and the back of the Wall; clay and rubble were used as filler for the core. Mortar was used very sparingly, typically only to position the facing stones. Today, the Wall requires constant monitoring and repair work for crumbling masonry.

This section also marked the most striking appearance yet of the Vallum (Latin for wall, which is a misnomer—the Anglo-Saxon monk Bede mistakenly identified it as an earthen wall some four centuries after the Romans left Britain. The correct Latin term for a ditch would have been "Fossa"[6]), the wedge-shaped defensive ditch built just to the south of the Wall that measured nine feet in depth while in use. It is speculated that the Vallum was built to help ward off attacks from Brigantes, a warlike tribe located south of the Wall in modern day Yorkshire. Another "idle hands are the devil's workshop" theory is that digging the Vallum was busy work for troops manning the Wall when there were no threats of attack. More than the actual Wall, the Vallum was a more constant feature for the rest of our trip, and it would serve as a reminder that we were walking close to the original fortification. It bobbed and weaved over the course of our hike, closely hugging the track of the original Wall in the lower elevations and retreating some distance from it when the Wall climbed the rocky ridgelines farther inland.

There was also a still visible ditch on the northern side of the wall, originally with berms on either side. On many long stretches of our upcoming walk along the highway, the road would feature the northern ditch on the right and the Vallum on the left. This northern ditch was also part of a hedgehog defense system of stakes, ditches and the Wall itself, with its defense network of forts, turrets and mile castles, manned at its peak by 15,000 men. It is easy to think of Hadrian's Wall as an extended standalone fortress, when it was in fact part of a complex militarized zone.

I marveled at how such an important section of archaeology, one that is designated as a World Heritage site, could be so hidden and unprotected. By contrast, a similar monument in the United States would charge admission and be advertised for miles on billboards next to the roads approaching the site with advertisements for tours led by locals dressed as Roman centurions. Dave, now released from his Monday morning investment pipeline call, could not resist the observation that the lack of promotion of the site was by no means unique in his experience and reflected "a combination of English reserve and a reluctance to seize on commercially lucrative opportunities."

Maybe I was being harsh at the time after mild irritation at three miles of going back on the previous day's hiking, but my thoughts turned to visits to the Berlin Wall which to this day is an industry in itself, and even the Great Wall of China which has, amongst other attractions, chairlift and toboggan rides. In a way the unspoiled nature of Hadrian's Wall is something to be valued and preserved, but one feels that more could be made of its history and status as a breakthrough ancient world military and engineering achievement without spoiling its historical appeal and authenticity.

The emperor Hadrian succeeded Trajan in 117 CE as emperor when Rome was at its height of imperial expansion. Hadrian's father was first cousin to Trajan (who later on his deathbed supposedly adopted Hadrian as a son), and this link, more than anything, secured Hadrian's claim as emperor. Hadrian was always considered somewhat of an outsider—his family came from a province in Spain (near modern day Seville), and he spoke with a Spanish accent his entire life. Hadrian was also gay and late in his reign established a cult religion celebrating his Greek lover, Antinous, who died tragically in a drowning accident on the River Nile.

The famous Roman historian Edward Gibbon described the 2nd century as "the period in the history of the world during which the condition of the human race was most happy and prosperous ... the vast extent of the Roman empire was governed by absolute power, under the guidance of virtue and wisdom. The armies were restrained by the firm but gentle hand of four successive emperors, whose characters and authority commanded involuntary respect. The forms of the civil administration were carefully preserved by Nerva, Trajan, Hadrian and the Antonines, who delighted in the image of liberty, and were pleased with considering themselves as the accountable ministers of the laws."[7]

Hadrian's ascension to Emperor came at a fortuitous time, just after the midpoint of the 200-year period known as the "Pax Romana" that started with the reign of Caesar Augustus and ended with the death of Marcus Aurelius in 180 CE. In the "Memoirs of Hadrian," a fictionalized account of Hadrian's life written by Marguerite Yourcenar, he acknowledged his good fortune: "the world which I inherited resembled a man in full vigor of maturity who was still fairly robust..."[8] Hadrian exemplified this confidence and virility in his interaction with the Roman army—he ate the same food, slept in the same barracks, and went on the same long marches as his troops when he showed up for one of his frequent inspections.

As flamboyant as he was in his personal life—he was the first Roman emperor to sport a beard and was both a passionate hunter and poet. Hadrian was conservative in terms of his plans for the Roman Empire. His focus was on consolidation of the empire and the introduction of a Romanized Hellenic culture in the conquered territories. The land known by the Romans as "Britannia" was the most far-flung province in the Empire, and evidence suggests that heightened military activity by the Caledonian hill tribes in the Scottish lowlands in 119–122 CE may have prompted his decision to build the Wall. It could have been considered a lower cost alternative to manned expeditions into Scotland to quell rebellions. In addition, the Wall was a barrier that could monitor the flow of people and trade in the region.

Peripatetic by nature—he spent more than half of his 21-year reign outside Rome visiting his provinces—he was in Britain in 122 CE when the six-year construction of the Wall had just been started, but he never returned to see the finished version.

A grand building project such as the Wall was completely consistent with Hadrian's love of architecture and grandiosity. He sought to recreate the most vivid memories of his travels to Greece and Egypt in the monuments constructed at the Tivoli villa near Rome. He also rebuilt the Parthenon in Rome as well as the theater in Corinth and completed one of the world's first urban renewal projects in London with the demolition and rebuilding (at twice the size) of the original basilica.[9]

Some of Hadrian's building schemes were not well received, most notably in Jerusalem, where he planned to replace the Jewish Temple with a shrine to Jupiter. A construction project next to Solomon's Tomb led to its collapse and was one of the proximate causes of the 132–136 CE Bar Kokhba Revolt that led to the destruction and diaspora of the Jewish people. After his victory, Hadrian changed the name of Judea to Syria Palestina.[10]

Only 10 years after its completion, Hadrian's Wall was temporarily de-commissioned—the decision was made by the Romans to move the protected border of Britannia 100 miles to the north, in the form of a turf and timber wall built by Hadrian's adopted son and successor as emperor, Antoninus. Hostile activity by the nine Celtic tribes identified by Romans in what is now modern-day Scotland (called "Caledonia" by the Romans), prompted the building of the earthen "Antonine Wall," which stretched for 40 miles from coast to coast across the narrow "wasp waist" of central Scotland.[11]

Only twenty years later, when Antoninus's adopted son, Marcus Aurelius became Emperor, the decision was made to pull back from the Antonine Wall and re-establish and reinforce Hadrian's Wall. This included completing the original 35-mile turf portion of the Wall from the River Irthing to Carlisle, which was replaced with stone.

Exhaustive research has been conducted and speculated about Hadrian's reasons for building the Wall. Rome expended tremendous resources manning the province of Britannia, which accounted for only 4 percent of the landmass of the Empire but required the commitment of 12 percent of its troops at its height. In the Roman psyche, Britannia always held a mystique and importance disproportionate to its strategic military value and its relative contribution to the overall wealth of the Empire. Julius Caesar's first military incursion into southern England in 55 BCE achieved little of strategic value but was met by a wild celebration in Rome and the Senate voted him 20 days of public thanksgiving, much more than was awarded to him after his vastly more significant military campaigns in Gaul.[12] Ancient Britain was unknown and steeped in mystery and required a naval armada of 100 ships to transport two legions across the English Channel; it was, in a sense, an ancient world equivalent of a moon shot that achieved enormous propaganda value.

The area that now comprises modern Scotland was constantly a thorn in the side of Roman rulers, so the Wall's presence had obvious intrinsic military value. One theory suggests that the decision to build the Wall was made after the "disappearance" of the IX Legion (Legio IX Hispana), which might have been annihilated in the beginning of the 2nd Century after advancing into Caledonia—the 2010 movie *Centurion* loosely followed this theory. Others believe that the legion was administratively dissolved, but there is a dearth of evidence as to its actual ultimate fate.

There were also strong commercial reasons for the Wall's construction—with gates positioned at every mile, the Romans were able to tightly control trade and collect taxes and duties. Building the Wall also kept three legions busy—not an unimportant consideration given the ever-shifting alliances that might threaten an emperor even in that relatively stable period of Roman history. Once the Wall was completed, the defense of it was largely left to auxiliaries and the three legions repositioned themselves to the south.

More than anything, the Wall may have represented a "shock and awe" level of technological accomplishment; a whitewashed bulwark clearly delineating where Roman civilization ended; beyond the Wall to the north, chaos and animal passions reigned. Similarly, on a smaller scale, the Romans built a bridge across the Rhine River in modern Germany to cow unruly Teutonic tribes. After pursuing the tribes deep into their forest sanctuaries, the Romans crossed back over the river and burned the bridge down. The Romans had made the devastating point—there would be no refuge for those who persisted in creating unrest on the fringes of its empire.

After leaving this stretch of exposed Wall, we passed through one of the few extended wooded areas along the Path. I was hoping to spot some wildlife, maybe a few squirrels, rabbits (introduced to Britain by the Romans), or even a badger or water vole as lovingly depicted in Kenneth Grahame's classic *The Wind in the Willows*. Unfortunately, the cumulative experience of unfortunate encounters with humans had taught these creatures to remain hidden while hikers trudged along the Path.

The small red squirrel, which I could always spot in the grassy mall style park in front of our London apartment, is in steep decline in Britain and in some danger of extermination. The culprit is the larger grey North American squirrel, introduced from the United States during the Victorian era, which has overrun the habitat of the native tree-dwelling rodent and now outnumbers it by twentyfold.[13] The future of the red squirrel has become so dire that several national and regional charitable trusts have been set up to help ensure its survival; 5,000 volunteers have been enlisted to help save the species, and they are taking measures such as culling the greys that are encroaching the red squirrels sanctuaries.[14]

The prospects of the unofficial English mascot, the hedgehog, have likewise plummeted. It is estimated that the country's population of the cuddly roly-poly mammals has declined by 95 percent since 1950. The proliferation of walls and fences has contributed heavily to their decline—hedgehogs routinely travel long distances to forage for food and find mates.

The post–World War II industrialization of farmland had driven most of the animals to the fringes, to the thatch and hedges on the peripheries of cultivated plots that were beyond the sweep of large tractors. The impact on wildlife has predictably been tragic—in the last 75 years, England has lost 95 percent of its wildflower meadows, 186,000 miles of hedgerows, and half of its wetlands.[15] Their habitats largely destroyed, the bird population saw reductions in 54 percent of its species; butterflies saw a 70 percent decline. Thirty percent of native plants saw a decline in their numbers in the last half of the 20th century alone.[16]

It has been suggested, somewhat controversially, that the industrialization of English farmland was accelerated by membership in the EU, which provided incentives to plough under unspoiled countryside to pay farmers for crops that "no one needed."[17]

At the end of World War II, Britain was one of the most sparsely wooded countries in Europe, and industrial farming further accelerated deforestation. Today, only an estimated 10 percent of the total landmass in England and 19 percent in Scotland are wooded. By comparison, 32 percent of Germany is forestland. In the three years I lived in London, the only time I was able to truly immerse myself in something approaching a deeply wooded sanctuary was a trip to the New Forest in Hampshire.

On the northern edge of Heddon-on-the-Wall, we came across another World War I monument to the fallen. This obelisk was a memorial to the 16 men from town that had died in the "Great War," as World War I is referred to in Britain. A rose was placed at the base of the statue, which was inscribed with the names of the local fallen—Knott, Armatage, Wright.... I always respected the British way of honoring the fallen of the Great War, which is largely forgotten in the United States; buried in popular culture by the drama and scope of the "Greatest Generation" of World War II. Arguably, the

Great War played a larger role than World War II in shaping the British psyche in the 20th century—the British death toll of the Great War exceeded that of World War II by over 200,000, and the perception exists to this day that World War I bled the nation dry by sacrificing the "flower of its youth." While living in London, I always made a point of buying a plastic poppy flower in November to help raise money for Remembrance Day.

I told Mark about my great uncle, Harry Western, a World War I soldier who fell in battle in Northern France in 1917 and who is commemorated in the same fashion on a military memorial in Arras, the capital of the Pas-de-Calais department of northern France and also on a memorial plaque at Exeter's St David's railway station honoring fallen soldiers who had been employees of the Great Western Railway. Some years ago I took my family and parents to Arras to view the memorial, pay our respects and pause for thought at what his life might have become. I also realized at the time that it was the first occasion when I had surveyed a war grave where, in this case through my grandmother, Harry's sister, I knew a close relative of the deceased. One day in 1917, with one tragic letter, arriving via the post, her brother simply ceased to be part of her life forever, and I can barely imagine her grief. And yet, having found his name on that memorial and spent a few moments in quiet contemplation, rather than feeling sad it impressed upon me that through his ultimate sacrifice and that of millions of others, how fortunate we are to live in the modern-day UK. It was a singular and life-affirming moment to have "found" him.

Years earlier, my family and I made a similar pilgrimage to a large American military cemetery outside of Florence to visit the memorial to my wife's uncle, a fighter pilot whose body was never recovered when he bailed out of his damaged plane in 1944 over Nazi occupied Italy during World War II. Like Dave, I found the act of visiting a foreign cemetery that held the remains of thousands of my countrymen to be an incredibly solemn and sobering experience.

For the next ten miles, our constant noisy companion was the busy highway, the B6318. This was originally the "Military Road," which was constructed in the mid–18th century after the Scots Highlanders, led by the Bonnie Prince Charlie, successfully invaded England. The main English army had been in Newcastle, and when the Highland army entered England through Carlisle on the opposite coast, the English could not respond—there was no east-west road that connected the 60 miles between the two cities.

After the Highland army was driven back across the border and ultimately destroyed at Inverness in 1745, the decision was made to build the Military Road, and stones were poached from Hadrian's Wall to lay the foundation for what is now a modern highway. For the fifteen miles from Heddon to Chollerford, we walked along the Military Road—built along the line of the original Wall—with the Vallum on the left and northern ditch on the right. Facing stones from the original Wall supposedly still appeared on the Military Road as recently as the early 20th century.

The areas we hiked adjacent to the road were wide fields populated by huge herds of sheep and cattle, and we were forced to negotiate fences separating different plots of land. This either involved opening and closing latched swinging gates or climbing over ladders and stiles. In some sections, the stiles would come in quick succession, every one-hundred feet or so, and it required a certain amount of dexterity to prevent an embarrassing fall into mud or cow or sheep dung. Similar to rooms in small English inns, every stile and ladder was unique in its own special way, which made climbing over them a bit maddening. They did, however, provide us with visible targets for competing the next section of the hike.

As a relative novice whose hitherto ambivalent attitude towards hiking prevented me from entirely shaking off the concern that I might at any time reach an inflection point and conclude that our coast-to-coast pilgrimage was a monumentally bad idea, I found this segmentation of the hike extremely helpful as a means of deflecting my attention from the vast distances, which we had to cover each day. More to the point, when I allowed myself to take in my surroundings rather than relentlessly "pushing on" I was reminded how much

I enjoy being in farmland and the uniqueness of the Path in facilitating an unbroken hike through a combination of agricultural land and open countryside. On top of that was the opportunity to follow the Path through several farmyards. I would probably confess to a somewhat rose-tinted view of agricultural life, but I can't deny how much pleasure I take from simply being physically present at any farm anywhere. Years of working in the London metropolis clearly had not done much to quell boyhood fascination with farm operations and machinery, as my gaze dwelt upon tractors, combine harvesters and even beaten-up road vehicles along our path. I was recently watching an old cooking program called Floyd on France, *where the late Keith Floyd, its legendary bibulous gastronome host, was describing farms he visited in Provence as "where trucks go to die." The comment was a perfect "visual" of farmyards for me. Wherever one goes, farmyards would be incomplete without at least one defunct agricultural vehicle or machine in situ. Emblematic as they are of hard agricultural toil, the average farmyard is none the worse for the presence of the odd mechanical relic of bygone harvests.*

The hard pavement alternated with squishy, waterlogged farmland that acted as suction on my soaked shoes and required extra effort to pull out and shove forward. My feet and legs were beginning to throb with pain, and we still had at least another ten miles to go.

We stopped at the Robin Hood Inn, a well-known pub and hotel situated next to the B6318. We needed a rest and drink, and we also took the opportunity to get our bearings on the remaining distance to our destination for the evening, the Red Lion Inn in Newbrough. I ordered a pint of bitter and asked the waitress how far we had to go, and she disappeared for five minutes before returning with pamphlet, which was a summary of Roman life in Britain. I had to inwardly laugh at her well intentioned but completely fruitless attempt to help—knowledge of the next meaningful landmark along the Path would seem to be a job requirement, particularly since the Robin Hood is one of the seven "stamping stations" for hikers who carried "passports" and wanted to earn a medal for completing the entire Path. This unfamiliarity with nearby villages and histori-cal points of interest was not uncommon in Britain—in rural areas; long-term residents may have no knowledge about a town only five to seven miles away. I always found this unapologetic insularity more amusing than frustrating.

Once we realized we still had almost ten miles to hike, we decided to skip lunch and quickly finished our drinks and pushed off. We continued to walk next to the busy motorway, but the sur-rounding landscape was lush and tumbling farmland, one that fea-tured cobalt skies, puffy white cotton ball clouds, huge wheels of golden hay and emerald turf, all framed by the clear blue waters of the Great Northern Lake reservoir, for as far as the eye could see. We periodically crisscrossed the road and climbed stiles as the Path meandered through the countryside. Nonchalant sheep and cows stood or rested on the turf close to the Path, and in some cases, refused to yield and shot us insolent looks when we skirted around them. Our constant and reliable guides were the "throwback" multi-directional wooden signs strategically placed whenever the Path changed course.

After climbing over yet another stile, I came across a pursed-lipped and furrow-browed Dave, whose path was blocked by a huge Holstein-Frisian cow.

Despite my early years spent in a semi-rural neighborhood in Gloucestershire, where my siblings and I frequently had to navigate our way through fields of livestock and what as a wee boy I referred to as "cow plop," I was initially at a loss to know how to safely edge past the stoic, unyielding cattle on narrow tracks. I remarked that it bizarrely but vividly reminded me of a tiny country bar in deepest Suffolk which I visited on holiday many years before, populated solely by a small number of sulky, four-square and unwelcoming-looking "locals," who fell stonily silent upon my entry. At first glance it actu-ally appeared like a cliché version of a quintessentially English coun-try pub situation. However, a welcome committee it most definitely was not, and the scene would not have looked out of place in Mark's

Farmland near Heavenfield (Mark Clegg).

beloved Midsomer Murders *TV series as a social gathering of local psychopaths and misanthropes. At the time I was carrying a candle lamp and was only looking for a box of matches, to enable me to get back to our cottage and find the electricity meter and could hardly have looked a threat to the neighborhood. Despite this, the atmosphere oozed xenophobia and the assembled malevolently muted locals immediately snapped back into animated conversation—as if somebody had found their "happy on-switches"—as I unlatched the bar door to make my somewhat relieved exit.*

After a brief discussion, I clapped my hands loudly. The cow continued to stare balefully at us, so we veered off the Path, safely outside of the radius of any possible back kick. The cow had not ceded an inch, and I hoped she took some satisfaction from her stubborn triumph.

___

Cattle along the Path are sometimes no laughing matter. They were a constant presence during our hike, and their sheer weight in numbers and complete disinterest in our plodding pace had the effect of making them appear innocuous. There have been bovine related injuries on the Path, including one man who was attacked in 2009 by an angry cow when he walked adjacent to her two calves. The protective mother charged the poor hiker, and he fell down while trying to escape, breaking his shoulder when he hit the ground. The injured man sued the landowner (and won) for lost earnings suffered as a result of his injury.[18] In 2015, a woman walking her dog near Brampton was trampled by cows and was airlifted to a hospital with critical injuries.

The local farmers also have to contend with tired or careless hikers who do not close gates behind them, allowing cattle to escape. The laws also require farmers to keep bulls out of land that is accessible to the public, so it is easy to understand why they do not always see the benefits of the Wall and the hikers who can not only be a nuisance, but also a legal liability.

My hikes in the United States cover trails in national or state parks and rarely traverse over even a small stretch of privately held land. It is a precarious balance between attracting tourists and keeping local landholders happy—particularly the ones who do not directly benefit from hikers. Stories abound of hikers who ask local homeowners to use the toilet or request food. One local landowner, who keeps sheep, said, "99% of them [tourists] are great. It's just the 1%. We've had Americans ask, 'Can we drive our car along the Wall?'"[19]

The ancient battlefield of Heavenfield abutted the northern side of the Wall, and a large cross was placed adjacent to it. This battle, fought in 634 AD, matched a Christian Northumbrian army against a pagan force of Welsh and Mercians (Anglo-Saxons from the south of England). The battle ended in victory for the Northumbrian King Oswald (who later attained sainthood), and his triumph was memorialized in the form of a small church that was consecrated on the

Late afternoon near Chesters (Mark Clegg).

adjoining slope (the original church is no longer standing). Oswald's martial glory, as was often the case in Dark Age history, was relatively short-lived. He died eight years later in battle, and his decapitated head was buried in Durham Cathedral.[20]

We passed Planetrees, which marked the spot where the Romans switched to the more narrow grade width for the remainder of the Wall, continuing westward until Bowness. This marked the high point of our walk for the day, and we started the 300 feet descent to the Chesters Roman Fort. One section of road led through a classic English sunken lane. Centuries of foot, horse carriage, and automobile traffic over soft limestone or sandstone surfaces created a recessed lane flanked by grassy slopes with swaying willows on both sides of the road reaching out and touching branches over the lane. The last of the early autumn sunshine filtered through the trees, scattering dapples of light along our path. I knew this moment, with the earth balanced between summer and fall in a timeless and unknown corner of Northumberland, would be etched in my memory forever.

We were both suffering from aching legs and feet as we covered the final miles for the day. Phone calls from work were interrupting Dave as we continued to alternate between farmland and pavement on our journey to Chesters.

We had a pre-arranged cab to take us the Red Lion Inn, and we called our driver at 5:30, one mile short of our planned rendezvous. Fortunately for us, we reached her just before she left for the day—if we had waited another 10 minutes, we would have had no other viable option of reaching our lodging, and we had no Plan B, except for possibly hitchhiking. She picked us up on a byway off the B6318, just before the old arched stone bridge over the North Tyne River.

It struck me during our slow drive to the hotel exactly how isolated we now were, just twenty or so miles from Newcastle. The Red Lion Inn in Newbrough is four miles from the Path, and we had passed nothing but small hamlets and farms during our 17-mile walk. I had read blogs on how difficult it was sometimes to find lodging and food along the stretch of trail from Heddon-on-the-Wall to Carlisle, and I had even recently read on Instagram about two young American women who were forced to abandon their hike when they could find no ATM machines along the route. Social media, primarily Instagram and Twitter, had been a great source of background material when I researched the Path in preparation for our hike. The ability to almost instantaneously exchange useful information with absolute strangers helped remove some of the uncertainty and isolation as we began the approach to the middle section of our trek.

Befitting its name, the Red Lion Inn is a classic old style English coaching inn dating back to the 12th century that fronts the main road into town, thereby ensuring that any travelers would spot the two-story limestone structure.

The Red Lion had six rooms, three on each side flanking the

The Red Lion Inn in Newbrough (Mark Clegg).

restaurant and pub. Although it was late September, the day had been warm, and I opened the window to my second story room. Newbrough is a small farming community, and I was immediately serenaded by the soothing sound of baaahing Blackface sheep through the open window. An occasional light breeze caused the lace curtains to flutter, adding to the tranquil rural ambience. I dozed in and out while watching an English soap opera on television.

Dave and I met up for dinner at the original stone and wood restaurant with a huge open fireplace. It was Monday, and a quiet evening in town, even by Newbrough standards. There was only one couple in the dining area.

As always after a long hike, I loaded up on protein and calories, in the form of Yorkshire pudding with gravy, chicken stuffed with haggis topped off with a parfait with meringue and berries. Back home, I do not typically eat such a meat intensive diet, but heavy physical exertion stimulates my carnivorous cravings. I spent half my time on the Appalachian Trail daydreaming about cheeseburgers.

Dave ordered a wine after dinner, and I once again randomly selected an artisanal gin. We reminisced about my time in London in the mid–1990s and remarked on how different the world was now. I recounted how I had met an American expat friend in a South Kensington pub in 1995, and we spent the evening gushing about the future of the United States; the Cold War had ended in the collapse of the Soviet Union, the stock market was soaring, and the government was on the verge of running budgetary surpluses. It was a classic "End of History" discussion based on the belief that the world was gradually becoming smaller and smaller as trade boomed and diversity was embraced. I felt like I was a microcosm of this borderless New Age and reveled in the fact that I was an American working in London for a Canadian bank with business coverage responsibilities in Germany.

I woke up in the morning to a beautiful early November morning after the 2016 presidential election feeling that my world had been broken and I had entered a parallel universe, where optimism, perhaps the most dominant characteristic of the American people since the country was formed, was replaced by a dystopian view of a menacing world—both inside and outside our borders. The words of the writer William Gibson have stuck with me—he had finished the manuscript of a new book on the eve of Trump's election but pulled it because he felt that his work was rendered irrelevant because the world that he thought he had known had disappeared.[21]

Similarly, the United Kingdom from my time there almost 25 years ago had begun to shake off decades of gloom and economic missteps and was setting forth on a course of new optimism. The UK was led back then by John Major, a prime minister who was so comically boring that he was correctly referred to as "The Grey Man" and pilloried on the satirical TV puppet show *Spitting Image* for a presumed obsession with garden peas. Major also made an appearance on the cover of *The Spectator*, the centuries old British satirical magazine, with the caption "The Snoreman Cometh." I never thought it would come to the point that I would yearn for ultra wary and colorless political leaders like George H.W. Bush and John Major, but three years of Trumpian chaos made me nostalgic for those politically dull and uneventful years.

I still somewhat viewed Britain through the prism of this mid–1990s time warp—Noel Gallagher of Oasis and the Cool Britannia image of the time, *Trainspotting*, Chelsea FC starting to play football with dash and verve, and the then anointed "golden theatrical couple" Emma Thompson and Kenneth Branagh.

I had spent the day before arriving in Newcastle walking around my old South Kensington neighborhood like a sad ghost, trying to retrace my steps past the mostly long closed shops and restaurants that I used to patronize. I ate alone at Khan's, my former "go-to" Indian restaurant, sitting at an outside table as the world whirled by with busy Londoners making their way back to work, school and in some cases, getting an early start to the weekend. Weighed down by jet lag, I stumbled to the Anglesea Arms, my old neighborhood pub (and the setting for my 1995 "End of History" discussion). My sense of direction had deserted me over the passage of time, and I got lost several times along the way. As one would expect, London had raced onward in the 25 years since I had left, and the changes had left me predictably bewildered and despondent.

Mark's reminiscence calls to mind an amusing moment around the turn of the millennium when we met in the same Anglesea Arms in South Kensington. He had travelled to London from the U.S. for a long weekend, and I arrived at the pub ahead of him and was nursing a pint whilst reading the sports pages and casting the occasional glance at the other pub-goers. I noticed a young lady standing on her own at one end of the bar cradling a gin and tonic, who appeared to have a permanently fixed smile as if she were suppressing laugher at a personal joke. The penny dropped when after some time, she drifted across the bar to a similarly-aged young man and asked, "Are you

'Sad Lonely Bastard 27'?" to which he replied, "Are you 'New Girl in Town'?" Apparently at that moment in history that was the contemporary way in which young people could meet as a result of online exchanges, with no identifying photographs but just a description, a location and an alias to go by. Of course, in the modern era the likes of Tinder make things all the simpler for singles, but it amused me to think about how developments in social media can so quickly transform accepted norms of human interaction. In a similar way, the experience of hiking the Wall had changed over the years with various social media platforms enabling the exchange of information and experiences as one progresses in a way completely removed from the days of my fell-walking youth when all one had as a guide would be a compass and, if you were lucky, a copy of one of Alfred Wainwright's beautifully illustrated walking guides.

Our server for the evening was a local young woman with long sandy colored hair pulled back in a ponytail and deep-set sapphire blue eyes. Since business was slow that evening, we talked for a while. She asked where we had traveled from that day, and we mentioned Wylam. She admitted she had never heard of it, much less ever been there, despite it being only about 15 miles away.

I once again found this insularity in the countryside of Britain alluring, a throwback to something so many of us had lost but could not quite identify—a sense of place and an accompanying lack of curiosity about what might lie on the other side of the ridge. For all I know, her dreams and ambitions might lead her to leave her ancient town and bolt to London at the first available opportunity, but I could not help to hope that the tug of home, still so unchanged, would always be strong.

It is all too easy for me and other city dwellers to be dismissive of the hopes and fears that accompany those isolated by geography, cultural inertia, or perhaps just a simple preference for a less complicated, slower paced life. Actual face-to-face encounters provide an invaluable counterweight to the paint-by-numbers caricatures as depicted by both traditional and social media. I was reminded of a quote decrying the worship of progress just for the sake of progress from one of Dave's favorite books, *The Road to Wigan Pier*, by George Orwell. "Notice the shrill wail of anger.... which meets the suggestion that his grandfather may have been a better man than himself; and the still more horrible suggestion that if we returned to a simpler way of life, he might have to toughen his muscles with a job of work."[22]

Dave mentioned that the experience of visiting small towns and staying in old country inns was a largely new one for him. On the surface, I found this astonishing, but I reflected on it and realized I was guilty of the very same shortsightedness—I always overlooked the harder to find treasures in my own backyard back home.

I went back to my room and stretched my aching body on the bed. The hike along Hadrian's Wall is touted as the easiest of England's National Trail walks, but the long distances between accommodations forces hikers to cover 15, 20, even 25 miles a day when detours are factored in. I briefly enjoyed the baaahing of the sheep until I realized that the unceasing ruminant racket was keeping me from nodding off. I got up and shut the open window.

Day Two was behind us and my initial fears of being defeated by the rigors of the Path were fast subsiding, assisted by another great pub dinner, lager "heart starters" and red wine. Life felt good and the more we chatted about old times, the more memories from Mark's time in London came back to me which until then had been long buried in a long-unvisited 1990s time capsule. Office characters and politics from the bank which we worked at, "liquid" office social events, and even a holiday when with our families we vacationed at St Simons Island, Georgia, all came up for discussion and the evening shot past quickly.

Despite mixed forecasts, the weather had so far been kind to us and I was now looking forward to what all of our pre-trip research had told us would be the most scenic stretch of our hike. I suppose that I was beginning to feel lucky and thought that we might completely dodge the bad weather. But luck, like English weather, is capricious, and our meteorological fortunes were about to change dramatically for the worse.

CHAPTER 3

Moorlands

One of the pleasures of hiking is the ability to justify the consumption of huge breakfasts, which we would rarely contemplate in our everyday lives. This day was no different and after a full plate of the local delicacy of Cumberland sausage, scrambled eggs, toast and coffee, we were picked up by the same cab driver who had dropped us off the previous evening. She agreed to drop us off (for an additional charge) at the same by-way where she had picked us up the previous afternoon. This left us about a one-mile walk along the Military Road over the famous 18th-century arched bridge that spanned the North Tyne River—the original Roman bridge had been constructed further downstream and had slipped into ruins centuries earlier.

As we entered the ruins of Chesters Roman Fort in Chollerford, a light rain began to fall. For the first time on the trip, I changed into waterproof pants and shoes.

Among the ruins were the remnants of the Roman baths, which were originally divided into a cold plunge room, a tepidarium (warm room) heated by an underground furnace system, and a hot steam room. Soldiers were provided three sets of shoes—boots for their uniforms, lighter shoes for indoors, and wooden soled shoes to protect feet from the hot surfaces of the bath. This would have been considered luxurious compared to the prevailing standards of that time, especially for the many soldiers who came from rural communities.[1] These shoes, along with other personal belongings of soldiers, are remarkably well preserved—the oxygen poor soil of northern England slows the decomposition of these priceless artifacts.

Although the Roman soldiers who built the wall were legionnaires (professional soldiers recruited from the Roman citizenry), those who manned Hadrian's Wall and its turrets and forts were largely auxiliaries—non-citizens from conquered territories. The Roman army relied heavily on auxiliaries offered as a form of tribute by defeated tribal chiefs. In addition to their skill as warriors, deployment of auxiliaries to remote and faraway Hadrian's Wall had the added benefit of reducing the likelihood of armed revolts back in their subjugated ancestral homelands. Service as an auxiliary offered many attractions—steady pay, food, and medical service, rounded off with a pension, land grants and Roman citizenship—also extended to common law wives—after 25 years of service.[2]

Training of both legionaries and auxiliaries was intense—they were forced to march 20 Roman miles with full gear, engaged in rigorous physical exercise such as running, jumping, and wall climbing, and they used mock battles to master their new weaponry.[3]

To commemorate the event, a bronze plaque was awarded to new auxiliary recruits who had completed their training, and some assumed Roman names to celebrate their new status. Many auxiliaries completed their first full length of service without engaging in major military campaigns—for instance, the Tungrian auxiliary units (from modern day Belgium) stationed at the town (vicus) of Vindolanda—located in Twice Brewed, a mile from the Path—had not participated in formal pitched battle since 83 CE. There were, of course, skirmishes and ambushes and punitive expeditions to punish unruly tribes north of the Wall, but no full-scale expeditions worthy enough to attract the attention of contemporary Roman historians.

In order to win citizenship, the auxiliary of course had to complete his 25-year service commitment. While death on the battlefield might have been a remote possibility, it is still estimated that just under half of auxiliaries finished their service—disease and infection killed many, and others were dismissed from their units due to injury.[4]

The climate in northern England from 100 to 300 AD was very similar to that of today or perhaps even slightly warmer and wetter—

warm enough to allow Romans to grow grapes in southern England that were used to produce wine.[5] According to the Greek historian Strabo, "Their (Britannia's) weather is more rainy than snowy; and on the days of clear sky fog prevails so long a time that throughout a whole day the sun is to be seen for only three or four hours round about midday."[6]

Hours of daylight ranged from eight per day in the early winter to seventeen at the summer solstice. Temperatures were cold but typically not unbearable in winter—many of the troops, particularly those from central Europe, would have found the northern English winters downright temperate compared to their experiences back home—and rain has always been a constant feature of Britain, although seldom reaching flood like extremes. Auxiliaries were adequately clothed along Hadrian's Wall, with cloaks for rain and long-sleeved tunics and trousers, underwear, and even socks, a true luxury for that era. In times of extreme cold, the troops would swaddle by layering on additional clothing.

There is considerable evidence that the soldiers along the Wall lived well, certainly much better than their Caledonian adversaries. The letters they wrote back home mention varied sources of food and drink. Analysis of sewage pits from Roman forces in the north of Britain show a diet that would be considered healthy by most contemporary dieticians, with a heavy concentration of grains, vegetables and fruit, including wheat, barley, raspberries, celery, apples, plums, peaches, grapes, and olives. For meat, Romans relied heavily on fish, shellfish, beef, mutton and local game, including boar, deer, and rabbit. For flavoring they relied on fish sauce, similar to the Asian version that is enjoyed today.[7]

The list of foods introduced by Romans to Britain is staggering: garlic, onions, shallots, leeks, cabbages, peas, celery, turnips, radishes, cherries and asparagus. Cultivated apple orchards were a Roman import, as were pheasants.[8]

For alcohol, soldiers stationed in "Romano Albion" relied mainly on vintners in Italy, Sicily, Spain and France for their wine supply.

Celtic beer made with barley malt is also mentioned in correspondence from soldiers posted at the Wall.

Britain also served as a source for key exports to Roman held territory in continental Europe. First and foremost, traders in Europe imported British metals, principally tin, copper and iron. No one is quite sure what motivated Julius Caesar to make his first military incursions into England in 55 BCE—punishing tribes in England that were assisting the Gauls in their wars in France against Rome seems to be the most popular theory—but securing tributes from local Celtic chieftains to supply Rome with these crucial metals would have to have been an important consideration.

Oysters from the Kentish coastline were served as delicacies at Roman feasts, and wild beasts from Britain were a source of entertainment in gladiatorial contests. A large industry devoted to glassware and pottery was also developed in England under Roman supervision. The huge amounts of coins have been dug up close to the Wall and in other parts of England attest to the trade and commercial opportunities available in Britannia.[9]

Auxiliaries for Hadrian's Wall were recruited or forced into service from all areas of the empire—modern-day Germany, France Syria, Iraq, North Africa, Spain, Romania, and, later, native Celtic Britons (although most Britons were sent to auxiliary units in continental Europe). Asturian cavalry from the northwest of Spain and Dalmatians from modern day Croatia were based at Chesters, and they, along with the other auxiliaries and centurions, gradually added their DNA to an already rich "English" genetic pool. More than 300 years ago, Daniel Defoe chided and satirized his countrymen for their xenophobia, particularly in light of their own mixed blood stock:

> Thus from a Mixture of all Kinds began,
> That Het'rogeneous Thing, An Englishman:
> In eager Rapes, and furious Lust begot,
> Betwixt a Painted Britain and a Scot.
> Whose gend'ring Off-spring quickly learn'd to Bow,

And yoke their Heifers to the Roman Plough:
From whence a Mongrel half-Bred Race there came,
With neither Name, nor Nation, Speech or Fame.
In whose hot Veins new Mixtures quickly ran,
Infus'd betwixt a Saxon and a Dane.
While their Rank Daughters, to their Parents just,
Receiv'd all nations with promiscuous lust.
This Nauseous Brood directly did contain
The well extracted Blood of Englishmen.[10]

Compared to the dangers that existed in other areas of the empire, life for the average soldier on the Wall approached some level of comfort. Daily needs were provided, and baths were an extravagance not readily available at home. Certainly there were dangers—the tribes north of the wall rarely launched full scale frontal assaults—although this sometimes occurred, most notably, in 181 CE and 367 CE—but they were an almost constant nuisance, and expeditions had to be organized to pursue raiders who somehow slipped past the Wall to thieve and plunder. These raiders, however, were typically weighed down by the booty from their incursions and were an easy mark for Roman cavalrymen seeking retribution. So while the risk of injury or death due to warfare was always present, the military force of the Romans was usually overwhelming, and once it could be gathered at a pressure point along the Wall or beyond, the native tribes were usually overmatched by the weaponry and skills of Roman soldiers and cavalry.

The Wall was not completely overrun by Picts until 367 CE, when the Roman Empire was entering the beginning of its terminal phase. Not only the Wall, but also much of the country was conquered as the northern invaders fanned out to the south and even threatened London. Even then in its weakened condition, with the emperor Valentinian distracted by events in Gaul, Roman control was quickly re-established and the invaders were driven back north in the following year. But, as is the case in our modern era, people motivated to circumvent physical obstacles, whether natural or manmade, will always find a way to do so, and while the Wall was not a sieve, it was hardly impermeable.

Based on modern culture's depiction of the Pict tribes—the name is derived from the Latin phrase *Picti,* meaning "painted ones" so named due to their numerous tattoos—in northern England and Scotland, it is easy to form the impression of the abject terror their appearance must have struck in those opposing them on the field of battle. Half naked with blue war paint, spiked hair and deadly two-man chariots with sharpened blades jutting from the wheel axles, their sheer outrageousness was designed to provoke fear and confusion, particularly against armies less organized and disciplined than the Romans.

While dismissive of their uncivilized behavior, the Romans, according to ancient historian Cassius Dio, held a grudging admiration for the resourcefulness of the Caledonians and their skill as warriors:

> They dwell in tents, naked and unshod, possess their women in common, and in common rear all the offspring. Their form of rule is democratic for the most part, and they are very fond of plundering; consequently they choose their boldest men as rulers. They go into battle in chariots, and have small, swift horses; there are also foot soldiers, very swift in running and very firm in standing their ground. For arms they have a shield and a short spear, with a bronze apple attached to the end of the spear-shaft, so that when it is shaken it may clash and terrify the enemy; and they also have daggers. They can endure hunger and cold and any kind of hardship; for they plunge into the swamps and exist there for many days with only their heads above water, and in the forests they support themselves upon bark and roots, and for all emergencies they prepare a certain kind of food, the eating of a small portion of which, the size of a bean, prevents them from feeling either hunger or thirst.[11]

What is perhaps less understood is how much the Romans, particularly their cavalry units, likewise inspired dread. Auxiliary cavalry along Hadrian's Wall rode stirrup-less upon large stallions bred in the southern reaches of the empire. The riders wore chain mail or heavy strips of articulated metal armor to protect the torsos, thighs, and shins. Menacing facemasks with openings for the eyes, nostrils, and mouth must have produced a psychological impact similar to American settlers facing Comanche horsemen wearing demonic war paint. Brass semicircular helmets called cooluses that protected the crown of the head were often fringed with long wigs made from reddish moss and topped with colored horsehair or goose-feathered crests. Cavalry units were led into battle by a standard bearer carrying a Draco, a long, horizontally positioned, hollowed out brass dragon that created a loud hissing sound when the cohort was at full gallop.

Underneath their armor, Roman troops wore woolen tunics colored crimson with dye created from the bodies of female Kermes insects endemic to the Mediterranean lands. Red was the color of Mars, the Roman god of war and also symbolized both blood and strength.

For weapons, Roman auxiliary cavalry were equipped with short spears, long swords (spathas) and javelins. For those Celts brazen enough to attack the Wall or conduct raids near it, the stampeding Roman equestrian warriors must have presented a terrifying combination of organized technical superiority, artistry, and death.

Perhaps the most chilling aspect of a Roman army march on a battlefield was the trained silence that accompanied the phalanxes remorselessly advancing on the enemy. This quiet engagement with Celtic fighters would have been unsettling in its own way, because it signified command of fear and emotions and was in sharp contrast to the war whoops and blood-curdling screams used by tribes north of the Wall. The drill orders, translated from Latin, were simple and effective: "Silence. Follow orders. Do not fall into disorder. Hold your ranks. Follow the standard. Do not leave the standard and pursue the enemy."[12]

The Roman units were organized with geometric precision. The century contained 80 men (not 100 as the name would suggest), led by an experienced, battle hardened leader called a centurion. The century was in turn divided into ten units of eight men apiece called a contubernium. These eight men slept together in the same tent or barracks room, depending on the situation. Six centuries comprised a cohort (480 men), and ten cohorts (4,800 men) represented the total number of fighting soldiers in a legion. Once supporting horsemen used as scouts and messengers, officers and other support staff were added to the mix, a legion's numbers swelled to 6,000 men.[13] The term "decimate" is derived from the Roman practice, during a civil war, to take eight men (drawn by lots) from each century of a mutinous army and execute them as a warning against future uprisings.

Most pitched battles from that era, extending into the Middle Ages, ended fairly quickly. After a barrage of javelins and arrows, two opposing armies would typically grind into each other clashing shields and using the cumulative weight of men to try and push the enemy backwards. Using their shields to parry sword and dagger thrusts while pushing and slashing until the other side sensed that things were not going well (almost always the tribes fighting the Romans) and the back rows would decide to break for it while there was still a chance for escape. At this point, the Roman auxiliary cavalry units would ride around from the flanks to chase down the panicked warriors in headlong retreat. They stood no chance against the mounted Roman forces, which butchered them as they gathered in small groups to make their final stands.

The full military might of Rome was launched against the Caledonians tribes in 208–211 CE in the "Severan Campaign," led by the African emperor Septimius Severus (up until the 1800s, there were many scholars who thought Severus, not Hadrian, had built the Wall). After assembling a force of over 50,000 legionnaires and auxiliaries, the Romans marched north of the Wall in a campaign of complete destruction. Before marching north, Severus spoke to his massed troops in York, issuing his "genocidal order" with quotes lifted from Homer and the *Iliad*: "No, we are not going to leave a single one of them alive, down to the babies in their mothers' wombs— not even they must live. The whole people must be wiped out of existence, with none to shed a tear for them, leaving no trace."[14]

The invasion of Caledonia resulted in an enormous loss of life on both sides and a brutality that we associate more with 20th-century "total wars" that inflicted misery and death on hostile forces and non-combatants alike—there is evidence, for instance, that captured Caledonians were herded into concentration camps south of the Wall. There is also evidence that the loss of life was so high in Caledonia that large swaths of land previously devoted to agriculture underwent reforestation after they were no longer cultivated.

Despite the huge amount of resources expended in both lives and disbursements from the treasury, the invasion of Caledonia also cannot be judged as a success for the Roman army. Although the tribes sued for peace after the first invasion in 208 CE, they were once again rebelling against Rome just a year later, and in 210 CE, Severus had to organize another massive campaign against the warring tribes. The strategic goal of subjugating, or even annexing Caledonia as a new province of Rome, had failed.[15]

The popular author George R.R. Martin has said that a visit to Hadrian's Wall was his inspiration for his five-book series, *A Song of Ice and Fire,* and its spin-off, the mega-hit HBO TV series *Game of Thrones.*[16] There are plenty of parallels between the history of the Wall and Martin's stories: a massive wall that stretches coast to coast, a northern, ginger-haired group of fiercely independent "Wildlings," and an outlaw, wifeless warrior caste (the "Night Watch") drawn from the far reaches of the empire (Westeros) that garrisoned the Wall. The panoramic attacks on the Wall as depicted in the TV series by the Wildlings mimic the military tactics used by the Caledonians, who gathered in forests some distance from the Wall to avoid detection—and the Roman auxiliaries—who lit beacons to alert other soldiers in distant Wall forts of an imminent attack.

"Moletown" was a village a short distance from the Wall in Martin's fictional series. Like Hadrian's Wall, where small towns ("vici") and marketplaces sprouted up to cater to the needs of the nearby soldiers, Moletown offered supplies and more illicit attractions such as gambling and prostitution to the lonely warriors stationed hundreds of miles from home. Loaded dice, forged coins, and even murdered bodies have turned up at excavations of vici located near the Wall. Life was, during this era, according to the Hobbesian quote, lived in a short, nasty and brutish manner, with average life expectancy of about 35 years. It is understandable that troops stationed at the Wall would want to seek the sensual pleasures of a vicus as temporary relief from the regimentation, drills, general boredom, and periodic violence that were part and parcel of their military service.

More than anything, the Romans forced civilization—the rule of law that guaranteed order, structure, and a rough version of equal justice—upon tribes fighting endless petty wars against other tribes in a perpetual cycle of violence with the inevitable retribution that it always sparked. This civilization at the point of sword, was, of course, accomplished by violence, certainly not a hallmark of reason or enlightenment, but it was the "stick" when the "carrot" was an ordered life that offered a refuge from the chaos swirling outside the borders of the empire.

We left the fort in the late morning and continued to walk westward, along the Military Road, entering the southern extremity of the Northumberland National Park. The rain was coming down heavier now; slanting down at a face first angle, and with slate grey skies blanketing the horizon, there was no prospect for a return to sunshine anytime during the day. Altogether, this was shaping up to be a day better spent in a village pub with a pint of bitter, a small crackling fire and a good book with great conversation and a fat tabby asleep on the windowsill, unbothered by the raindrops gathering on the other side of the lead paned glass.

The Path ran through bleak, featureless terrain parallel to the motorway, and it was becoming more slippery by the hour. I had left my hiking poles at home—I was restricted to carry on luggage on my flight to London—I was a non-paying standby passenger, courtesy of Delta Airlines, where my daughter is employed—because airport security would consider my aluminum hiking poles potential weapons. I had no way to steady myself when the inevitable patch of slick

Spider web holding raindrops on hike to Housesteads (David Wilmot).

mud caused me to lose my balance and slip and fall backwards. There were luckily no hard surfaces around, so I had a soft landing that left me unhurt beyond my injured pride. After taking stock of the situation and realizing I was unscathed, I slowly pulled myself up and continued to slog through the rain.

Mark's first fall certainly gave me a moment. He is what we call a "big lad" and his heavy crash momentarily made me wonder how on earth I would get him off the hill if he were hurt. There were very few people on the hike and it gave me pause for thought as to how quickly any medical services could get to us in case of need (always a consideration for me given my talent for breaking bones whilst participating in such supposedly limited-impact sports as cricket and jogging). Sometime after our hike I saw a promotional video for the recent invention of a rocket-powered suit intended for Air Ambulance paramedics to use in rescuing stricken hikers in remote locations, and which was being trialed in the Langdale Pike area of the Lake District. Whilst literally comic book in appearance, perhaps it will over time bring a new dimension to mountain rescue efforts.

I was surprised by my fall—this happened frequently during my hikes in the mountains, when I would trip over a tree root or make a misjudgment like placing my foot on a slick, moss covered rock. But the terrain here was not nearly as treacherous, and I had no good excuse or explanation for my misstep—I was even more surprised, when, an hour later, I slipped and tumbled to the ground again.

I later scoured accident reports of hikers along the Path, and somewhat unsurprisingly, learned that they happen with a fair amount of frequency, including one death in early 2019. Like most people, I tend to relax my guard when the terrain is relatively flat and the path ahead is straight for a far as the eye can see. Benign topography reduces the frequent downward glances that would normally reveal the little booby traps—a gray slick of mud or patches of wet grass—that can cause a twisted ankle or a trek-ending tumble.

In anticipation of a fairly easy hike, I also had not planned properly in terms of my gear—no hiking poles, no poncho, and the biggest omission, no waterproof gaiters to cover my shoes. Even more importantly, I had not prepared physically or mentally for a hike that was demanding in its own unique ways. It was certainly not difficult from a cardio-vascular standpoint; I was not experiencing any of the shortness of breath and spikes in blood pressure that I was accustomed to from my higher elevation mountain hikes in the United States. But mountain hikes almost always offered a welcoming place to sit and rest in the form of a crude bench or even a felled log. There was almost nowhere along the Path to sit and rest, to have a drink of water and pore over a map. The Path marched on relentlessly onward, and its regularity, except for interruptions by stiles and ladders, lured us constantly onward, and we rarely paused, even for something as essential as a snack or a drink of water.

Dave seemed to be coping with the rigors of the Path a bit

better—he had trained for the hike at his gym in London, and he was powerfully built, with a lower center of gravity. He was beginning to walk ahead of me by a hundred meters or so, which did not bother me in the least. He was also able to spend a fair amount of time on the phone with a colleague in Munich, finessing multi-million-dollar deals while slogging his way through the soaked ground of Northumberland. He later told me that at the other end of the phone his colleagues in Munich, Paris and London could clearly hear the percussive beat of the incessant rain against his nylon hood as he tried to protect his smartphone from the downpour while pitching his deal. I was not the slightest bit competitive about maintaining the same pace with another hiker and had always lived by the famous Appalachian Trail mantra "hike your own hike." In a certain sense, I preferred the independence that came with the separation from a fellow hiker. It probably also helped to know that every day we were hiking with a shared objective of a good dinner, adult "bevvies" and more wide-ranging conversation once we reached our daily destinations.

I was mindful of Mark's "hike your own hike" advice but the reality was that my maintenance of a steady, reasonably quick pace was the best, and perhaps the only means of combatting the stiff and aching muscles in my legs. This pain was exacerbated by the increased number of steep climbs in this section of the Path and the progressively worsening climactic conditions. After two benign days, the uncompromising wind and rain was finally coming for us in a big way and reminiscent of the "good anti Grand Slam weather" I had experienced many years before on that biblically rainy Sunday afternoon in April in Edinburgh. The views on the Path were very different to Edinburgh's and often breathtaking, but the rainfall statistics were regrettably similar in their scale.

We were gradually gaining elevation as we began our ascent into the middle portion of the Path, and the landscape had shifted from verdant farmland to the bleak moors associated with the Pennines, the long, 268-mile north-south chain of limestone hills and mountains which run from Derbyshire in the middle of England to the Scottish border. The rocky soil was not suitable for cultivation; the pastures of sheep and cattle that we were so accustomed to were slowly disappearing as we labored past heather and the occasional solitary sycamore or rowan tree.

Visibility was rapidly diminishing as we climbed upward and skirted Limestone Corner, a ditch filled with quarried stones that the Romans had discarded, presumably because hauling them to the higher peaks along the Wall was not, upon further reflection, worth the required Herculean effort. Limestone Corner is also the north-ernmost point on the Wall, but the rain and low cloud cover dashed any hope of viewing the distant Cheviot Hills and Scotland in the distance.

We crossed back over to the south side of the B6318 and continued on marshy footpaths bordered by knee-high and drenched moor grass. We ate a quick lunch in Carrawburgh, next to the remains of the Mithraeum, a temple of the mystery religion of Mithras, which was a widespread, clandestine religion that had many followers in the Roman army at the time the Wall was built.

Believed to have originated in Persia, not much is known about the tenets of the faith—its followers strictly obeyed its emphasis on secrecy. With its successive grades attainable through achievement and promotion, highly secretive rituals and hierarchies, many believe it provided the foundations for Freemasonry.

The temple remains were at the southwestern corner of the Roman fort. Only the earthworks still remained from the fort; the stones had been hauled away long ago to help build the adjacent Mil-itary Road—the current columns are replacements, carved and chis-eled to resemble the originals. The auxiliaries who had manned this fort came from modern day Germany, The Netherlands, and France.

The temple was subterranean, meant to resemble the cave where the Creator and Sun God Mithra (or Mithras)—born on December 25 under the sign of a star—had slaughtered a primeval bull. In his death, the bull's life forces were released, in the form of body, blood and semen, thereby creating life on earth. This triumph over the bull

Wiregrass along the Path (Mark Clegg).

would have been memorialized at the altar of the original temple in the form of a tauroctony, a bas-relief that would have depicted the battle.[17]

The worshippers of Mithra were stargazers, and the constellation Taurus would have been at its most prominent phase during the spring equinox 2,000 years ago. Thus, the onset of spring and new life would have coincided with the emergence of Taurus (the Bull) in the northern night sky, before yielding to Aries, the Warrior, who arose in April, and represented the slaying of the bull.

Mithraism stressed the eternal verities of loyalty, bravery, benevolence and obedience, and these virtues would have squared up well with the values of the Roman Army. It is easy to understand why lonely auxiliaries, hundreds and even thousands of miles from home would have adopted and embraced this secretive religion as a bulwark, a refuge, in a bleak and remote corner of the Empire. The mere fact that Mithra was the Sun God in a land where the sun was frequently blocked by clouds or blanketed in darkness during the dismal winter months would provide further incentive to adopt the mystery religion.

Rudyard Kipling evoked the spirit of Mithras and its appeal to a lonely soldier stationed at the extremity of empire:

> *Mithras, God of the Morning, our trumpets waken the wall!*
> *"Rome is above the Nations, but Thou art over all"*
> *Now as the names are answered, and the guards are marched away,*
> *Mithras, also a soldier, give us strength for the day!*
>
> *Mithras, God of the Noontide, the heather swims in the heat,*
> *Our helmets scorch our foreheads; our sandals burn our feet,*
> *Now in the ungirt hour; now ere we blink and drowse,*
> *Mithras also a soldier, keep us true to our vows!*
>
> *Mithras, God of the Sunset, low on the Western main,*
> *Thou descending immortal, immortal to rise again!*
> *Now when the watch is ended, now when the wine is drawn*
> *Mithras also a soldier, keep us pure till the dawn!*
> *Mithras, God of Midnight, here where the great bull dies,*
> *Look on thy children in darkness. Oh take our sacrifice!*

Many roads Thou has fashioned: all of them lead to the Light,
Mithras, also a soldier, teach us to die aright [18]

Those who view Kipling through a 21st-century lens have largely discredited him as a bandleader for imperialism. But this poem is both timeless and meditative—it beautifully expresses the weariness and fears of a Roman soldier stationed on the Wall, captured within the context of the arc of a day and evening as metaphors for life and death.

The Romans were very tolerant of those who chose to worship gods other than their own as long as they also paid respect to the Roman pantheon of pagan deities. Both early Christianity and the Druidism practiced in Britannia demanded fealty to their own god(s) to the exclusion of all others. It is thought that a local Christian commander desecrated the Mithraeum in Carrawburgh in the early 4th century CE after the emperor Constantine declared Christianity to be the state religion.

Christianity never succeeded in becoming a monolithic religion in Roman Britain. It was always practiced more by the ruling classes and in the towns, but it did not hold much sway among the general population. Various forms of paganism and Mithraism enjoyed strong comebacks in the latter half of the 4th century CE, and the structure of Christianity in Britannia collapsed when the Romans departed. It only gained a significant foothold in Britain through the work of Irish missionaries who arrived late in the 5th century CE, almost a century after the Romans had departed.

At the far end of the Mithraeum, next to where the bas-relief would have been chiseled, hikers had left tokens in the form of coins and candles. A German hiker, a lady whom we had met earlier, arrived and pointed out this makeshift memorial. We mused aloud about what Mithraism might have represented, and she shrugged and said, "power, just like all religions." We chuckled at her terse but accurate comment and headed back up the Path.

I have always enjoyed "walking alongside history." During my time in London, I would walk across London Bridge twice each working day, from Monument tube station to my office in Southwark each morning, and back again in the evening. There was not a single time I made this crossing that I did not reflect on the fact that I was actually walking over London Bridge (even if it was not the original, medieval version) and that always made me smile inwardly.

Similarly, when we would travel to the West Country, I would take walks along the paths and fields where the fictional characters in Thomas Hardy's novels traversed and explore the beautiful battlefield near Hastings in Kent where William the Conqueror defeated the English army of King Harold in 1066. We hiked along the wind-swept cliffs of the northern Cornish coast and through the misty mountains of Snowdonia in north Wales, transfixed by the varied landscape and the rich histories of each place we visited.

The rain came down harder, pounding us with cold, stinging pellets. We continued to slowly climb upward, reaching an elevation of about 1,000 feet as we hiked through the fog past the Sewingshields Crags. This area marked the sheerest drop off of the hike—the remnants of the Wall hugged the cliffs, which needed no northern facing ditch when invaders from that direction would have had the impossible task of scaling the steep crags. In addition to the 16 forts built south of the fortification, the Romans also built "milecastles," small fortlets that were embedded in the Wall that also served as gateways allowing authorized ingress and egress. In between each milecastle were two, three or four story turrets, manned by small groups of soldiers. These turrets served as watchtowers that provided an early warning system for suspicious activity north of the Wall and were connected by wall curtains that allowed for movement of troops along the top to reinforce stress points during attacks. There were two such turrets built along Sewingshields Crags, which was a remarkable feat of engineering given the rocky topography and high elevation along this segment. But the Romans prized linearity above anything else, and this pattern was repeated (two turrets between each milecastle) for the entire Wall with only one exception, at Peel

Gap, where there are three turrets between the two milecastles.[19] Roman soldiers could spot approaching groups from the north miles before they reached the Wall. Rather than crouch defensively on the ramparts, soldiers and cavalrymen would typically open the gates and meet the advancing Caledonians before they reached the Wall.

I had also noticed on my menu from the Red Lion the previous evening a selection for Sewingshields steaks. Now I knew the provenance for that no doubt delectable meal, although I did not spot any unfortunate livestock in the area.

As we continued our trek through the rain with feet now soaked by thousands of steps through the waterlogged Path, both of our phones pinged, in quick succession, with special news announcements.

Back home, House Speaker Nancy Pelosi had announced the formal impeachment inquiry of President Donald J. Trump for his role in dangling financial inducements to the Ukrainian government in exchange for supplying "dirt" on Joe Biden, his presumed opponent in the 2020 presidential election. In Britain, the UK Supreme Court had voted, by a margin of 11–0, against the legality of Prime Minister Boris Johnson's "proroguing," the suspension of Parliament for most of the period leading up to the planned Brexit date of October 31.

The Supreme Court ruled that "this Court has already concluded that the Prime Minister's advice to Her Majesty was unlawful, void and of no effect."[20] *This debate raged on in the online media as we continued on our path. It was a field day for political commentators and the spectrum of opinions across the country ranged from Boris "needing to do the decent thing and resign" to "the judiciary should keep out of Parliamentary matters." Once again, the Brexit-driven national divide manifested itself, as the UK political environment continued to be dominated by inconclusive and emotionally charged commentary. Just to accentuate the political chasm, there was a significant body of opinion in favor of holding a second referendum, which compounded the all-consuming and suffocating lack of any direction and conclusion being in sight. As we walked through the harsh Northumbrian weather conditions, which had quickly deteriorated from what the Scots refer to as "dreich" (gloomy, overcast) to "drookit" (think A Perfect Storm), the hiking analogies were working overtime. It was as if the UK was a hiker trying to complete the Path in thick fog, wearing lead boots, and with no white acorns to mark the way to the ultimate destination. I had some sympathy for the politicians in Westminster—the referendum outcome had been clear but the route to the exit seemed to be riddled with political, legal and administrative quicksand. It put me in mind of the Talking Heads song "Road to Nowhere." Indeed our seemingly endless and progressively drenched slog that day towards our destination seemed to have more direction and momentum than events in Westminster. One immutable fact was that the further we travelled on our slow but determined progression westwards on that dreich/drookit Monday, the more we increased the geographic, if not the "share of mind" distance from the battleground at our political epicenter at the House of Commons. Against this our westward hike and the rain took on a soothing quality.*

My Twitter feed was exploding with one "hot take" after another about these twin developments, and I smiled inwardly at the juxtaposition between these events and the slower moving but equally impactful political rumors and news from distant points in the Empire that likewise must have frightened and even amused the defenders of the Wall almost 2,000 years ago. Civil wars were common throughout Roman history, and Roman generals would have needed to keep abreast of events in the capital as ambitious men, backed by government or privately raised armies, vied for control whenever a power vacuum arose. The jockeying for power amongst different factions within the Roman Army during times of internal strife would have been impactful for even the lowest soldier in the most far-flung reaches of the Empire.

Dave and I spent a few minutes reading aloud quotes from red-hot social media feeds feasting upon the bizarre parallels between political events on either side of the Atlantic. It was clearly shaping up to be a bad press day for both national leaders, with plenty of debate about which of the two members of the "special relationship" had come out of it the worst.[21] We are both (much derided) baby-boomers, and as such, had taken a stable and increasingly democratic world as a given. It was the system delivered to us by our parents and grandparents through their participation in wars and wrenching but ultimately beneficial economic disruptions, and it only made sense that this progress would continue in a linear manner. It would be a prosperous and tolerant world that we would bequeath to our children and their children. The historical populist and nationalistic animal spirits in the West were a product of a bygone era, as national borders and tribal urges would inevitably give way to a peaceful and thriving world made smaller by technology and shared norms. Children in Beijing would buy Los Angeles Lakers or Man City jerseys and we would teach our kids Mandarin and visit each other's tourist attractions and eat each other's food and watch each other's movies in a never-ending cycle of mutual cultural absorption.

We were as naïve as Roman citizens had been when their Republic was a model for governance in the ancient world. The Roman Republic was by no means as democratic as the governments we enjoy to the present day in most of the West. Oligarchic patrician families who had enjoyed power for centuries dominated the Roman Senate, and more often than not, they sought to limit direct democracy. Voting was restricted to citizens, and as recently as 100 BCE was not even extended to many land-holding male—females were eligible for citizenship but never had the right to vote—inhabitants outside of Rome on the Italian peninsula.

For most of its first three centuries leading up to the defeat of Hannibal and Carthage during the Second Punic War in 202 BCE, the Roman Republic had been led by a small group of elite families who valued, above all else, honor, patriotism and glory. Roman citizens were expected to "temper their competitive instincts" for the greater good of the people.[22] This selflessness did not restrict wealth accumulation and even concentration among powerful, legacy families, but obtaining riches in and of itself was not nearly as prestigious as honorable (typically military) service to the Republic.

The increasing wealth of Rome, made possible by its imperial conquests in North Africa, the Middle and Near East, Greece and other areas along the rims of the Mediterranean and Black Seas, led to an explosion in wealth after Hannibal was defeated in the Second Punic War in 202 BCE.

Riches emanating largely from precious metals and slaves flowed in from the conquered territories and led to widespread corruption, as *publicani* appointed by the Roman Senate were contracted to collect taxes in the provinces. The Roman Treasury agreed to a set sum to be collected by the publicani, and anything above this amount the publicani were allowed to retain. Naturally, the taxes collected far exceeded the amounts remitted back to Rome.[23]

As the plunder from conquered territories made its way back to Rome, the competition for command of armies—required for the forceful acquisition of riches—amongst senators grew fierce. This led to widening gaps in wealth between the more affluent politicians, who were increasingly supported by both private and government armies, and the poorer senators, who were unable to bankroll their political careers.

The super wealthy and politically connected won the contracts for the massive infrastructure projects undertaken during the 2nd century BC in Rome. Craftsmen and farmers from rural areas flooded into the capital to find steady work, and the population grew from about 200,000 at the end of the war with Hannibal to 500,000 just 70 years later. By 186 BCE, as many as one-third of the inhabitants of Rome consisted of immigrants, and "the city was burdened by a multitude of people from abroad."[24]

Corruption, wealth inequality, and a flood of immigrants led to the inevitable populist backlash. The dishonest behavior of the elites had left a vacuum that opportunistic politicians with outsized personalities filled, usually by skirting the long-established laws and norms of the Republic to push through popular measures such as land reform and the confiscation of large estates. While a large portion of the population supported these reforms, they were forcefully implemented through violent and extralegal means, which led to civil wars and the granting of temporary emergency powers to dictators. The politics of duty and honor during the earlier days of the Republic had been supplanted by personal advancement, corruption, and greed.

By the time that Hadrian assumed power in 117 CE, the Roman Republic had not existed for almost two hundred years—it had been replaced by a series of emperors from Augustus Caesar, to Hadrian's predecessor and first cousin, Trajan.

We continued our walk through the mist, hugging the crags on our right as we made our way to the Roman fort of Housesteads, perched near the top of an 800-foot hill. The climb in elevation revealed impressively preserved portions of original Wall. The manpower required to poach and transport stones from this hard-to-reach section of Wall in the mid–18th century to build the now distant Military Road must have been prohibitive, which played no small role in ensuring that this remote stretch remained relatively intact. Along the way, we crossed Busy Gap, site of a road that passed through the then still formidable Wall ruins during medieval times. "Busy Gap rogues" referred to cattle thieves or reivers who operated with impunity in this border region between Scotland and England, from 1400 to 1700.[25] The legend of the reivers has continued into the present day with, for example, the establishment of the Border Reivers rugby union team in the Scottish town of Galashiels in 1996.

Due to its remoteness, distance from London and fiercely independent populace, the border country was allowed by The Crown to operate in a largely lawless and uncontrolled environment. The crime of "rustling" was a descriptive term for stealing cattle; "reiving" (a Scottish word for thieving) referred to the border country practice of stealing from neighbors.[26] William Faulkner's novel *The Reivers*, published some two centuries after the border country migration to America began, featured three car robbers from Mississippi.

Section of Wall near Housesteads (Mark Clegg).

There were four major regional migrations from Britain to America in the first two centuries after the English first settled in Virginia in 1607: the non-conformist religious orders such as the Pilgrims and Puritans who largely came from East Anglia and settled in New England; the landed gentry loyalists to King Charles I from the West Country of England, who left during the reign of Oliver Cromwell and settled in the Chesapeake Bay region; the Quakers, who originated largely from the English Midlands and settled in the Delaware Valley; and the border country immigrants from northern England and the southern Scottish lowlands who settled in Appalachia.[27]

The sense of isolation on this section of the hike along the border country—described as "high moorlands of almost lunar bleakness"— would have been even more pronounced three centuries ago.[28] The people who populated the region in the 18th century were largely poor tenant farmers. They combined their poverty with a fierce pride that resisted subordination to both governmental and religious central authorities.

Their ancestors (and mine—my father's branch of the family emigrated from northern England in the late 17th century) played on outsized role in the electoral politics of the United States, which started with President Andrew Jackson, a Carolina backcountry politician of Scots-Irish and border country origins—most of the English and Scottish Protestants who settled in Ulster in the 17th century emigrated from the Scottish lowlands and northern England—who successfully led the first populist revolt in America against the established cultural elites from Virginia, New York, and New England. The Appalachian supporters of Jackson were defined by a reflexive cultural conservatism, an inclination to violence, xenophobia, and a resistance to authority. "In the early nineteenth century, they tended to detest great planters and abolitionists in equal measure. During the Civil War, some fought against both sides. In the early twentieth century they would become intensely 'negrophobic' and anti–Semitic. In our own time they are furiously hostile to both communists and capitalists. The people of the southern highlands have been remarkably even-handed in their antipathies—which they have applied to all strangers without regard to race, religion, or nationality."[29]

Most of the immigrants from the border country to the United States came from unprivileged backgrounds and were tenant farmers or semi-skilled craftsmen. Their social betters in New England and Virginia looked down upon them, but this sniffing disdain from others did not quell their fierce pride—"Border emigrants demanded to be treated with respect even when dressed in rags. Their humble origins did not create the spirit of subordination, which others expected of 'lower ranks.'"[30]

The surnames of the north British border country settlers are dotted throughout the history of the United States, including 18 presidents, ranging from Andrew Jackson to James Knox Polk (whom

I am distantly related to), Theodore Roosevelt, Woodrow Wilson and Ronald Reagan.[31] The first man to step on the moon, Neil Armstrong, and the world's most renowned modern evangelist, Billy Graham, had roots in the border country.

The border country immigrants brought to America such practices as clay and wattle daubed log cabins and "cowpens," corrals with a stockade built for protection of family members and livestock when attacked. The well-known Battle of Cowpens occurred during the Revolutionary War in the South Carolina upcountry.[32] The most common British county name in Appalachia is Cumberland, the erstwhile name of Cumbria, and there is a Northumberland County and a city named New Castle in Pennsylvania.

Speech patterns from the border country made their way across the Atlantic Ocean and found a new home in the Appalachian Mountains—the use of double negatives ("I never sold none"), fixing (for getting ready), and let on (to tell) are just a few examples.[33]

The descendants of the border country and Scots-Irish settlers—along the spine of the Appalachians from Pennsylvania and southeastern Ohio down to northern Alabama—provided the backbone of the nativist revolt that allowed Donald Trump to eke out victory in 2016. Their national electoral clout shows no signs of dissipating in the near future given the disproportionate representation afforded to sparsely populated states through the U.S. Senate and Electoral College.

We made it to the famous hill fort complex of Housesteads in the mid-afternoon. Unlike the other ruins at Chesterfields and the Mithraeum, fencing surrounded the sprawling east-west Housesteads fort complex. Those wishing to walk amongst the ruins had to enter the nearby visitor's centre and pay for admittance.

Housesteads was another example of the somewhat ad hoc nature of the Wall's construction—a completed turret had to be torn down shortly after its construction to make way for the fort, which garrisoned over 1,000 troops of the Roman (Augusta) Second Legion and auxiliaries, most of whom came from modern day Belgium and Germany.

Unlike the other ruins we had visited thus far, the buildings were (absent roofs) still fairly intact at Housesteads, which made it easy to visualize a fort containing all the necessary structures needed to house, feed and store the supplies for the soldiers stationed at the five-acre stronghold.

The rain continued to spit from the grey skies as we trudged around the sodden turf of the complex. My "waterproof" hat, jacket, pants and shoes were no longer repelling the rain. I was reminded— having first learned through my experience hiking the Appalachian Trail—that there is no such material that is waterproof after a certain point of saturation.

We made our way past the fort's headquarters, called the "Principia," which featured the Roman version of central heating using hot air rising from fires burning in the floor below to the latrines, the Romans favored communal toilets for its military, and the phrase "the wrong end of the stick" originated from this practice. A slave would typically hand a stick with a sponge end to a Roman soldier, who would use it to wipe. When not in use, the stick was kept in a bucket of salted water. It is not difficult to understand how this phrase was derived, and if a mistake in handling the stick was ever made, it was unlikely to ever be repeated.

The rain ended our tour of Housesteads earlier than we would have liked, and we went back into the visitor center for drinks and snacks. The kindly woman in charge of the small complex gave us directions and an estimate of the remaining distance—about two and a half miles—to Once Brewed, our destination for the evening.

This stretch of the Path is referred to as the "Clayton Wall," named after the 19th-century archaeologist John Clayton, who actually owned Housesteads and four other forts along the Path. Clayton belonged to a distinguished line of English "gentlemen" amateur archaeologists, who conducted their research and excavation efforts when time permitted (Clayton worked as a town clerk in Newcastle) at their own expense. Under Clayton's supervision, the Wall was reconstructed along this segment, and it can be distinguished from the original Roman version by the lack of mortar and a turf top.[34]

As we walked next to the Clayton Wall, perhaps the most photographed section along the Path, I visualized the lonely auxiliary looking north from a turret, scanning the grey rainy skies for any sign of an encroaching enemy. His predicament was captured perfectly in the sonnet couplets of "The Roman Wall Blues," a poem in the famous W.H. Auden *Twelve Songs* compendium about a hardened, one-eyed Tungrian (Belgian) veteran stationed at the Wall who speaks of the cold wet wind (which induced a head cold), lice in his tunic, and the incessant rain.

His thoughts reflect an existential weariness—he bemoans not only his bone deep physical discomfort; he also questions the very significance of a life dedicated to military service to a foreign power in a foreign land, all the while brooding over his girl back in Tungria—soldiers of a lower rank were forbidden to marry—whom he has not seen in years.[35]

This poem is unremittingly bleak, and it suggests that the soldier will not derive anything positive from his experience at the Wall, and "do nothing but look at the sky," when he is older and retired from military service. His life on the border of Britannia and Caledonia would have been filled with long stretches of mind-numbing drills and guard duty boredom, interspersed with brief moments of fear and violence. Maybe Auden visited the Wall on a mercilessly wet, late September day like the one I was experiencing; it would have made it easier to imagine not only the physical discomfort of the auxiliary, but also to register his creeping dread of the shorter days and colder, wetter, and windier weather yet to come.

As another year ebbed away, maybe the solitary auxiliary could spot the smoke curling up into the grey sky from the Celtic circular huts a safe distance from the Wall; catch a whiff of roasted meat from their open pits when the wind blew in from the north; hear the rumble of chariots or the raucous shouts as they celebrated the festival of Samhain, when on the first of November, the veil was briefly

Housesteads fort (Mark Clegg).

pulled back between the world of the living and the realm of the dead. Maybe he found comfort in the arms of a Pict woman in the nearby vicus south of the Wall whose embrace let him briefly forget the ache of separation from his girl in Tungria while he raised a Celtic beer toast in memory of his lost comrades. Or he roared with laughter in a game of dice when he won a month's wages after wagering a bet against a new arrival to his cohort

We walked along the Path leading to Milecastle 38, site of the infamous *Dutch bankers* affair in 2003. In January of that year, when the ground was at its most saturated from rainfall, AMRO Bank (whom I had coincidentally been employed by earlier in my career) decided to conduct a team building exercise with 850 employees hiking the stretch of Path between Housesteads and Steel Rigg. The intent was to use the iconic backdrops of the Wall Path as an inspirational message to its staff.

There had been some communication with Wall Path authorities prior to the visit, but logistics were never quite agreed to—trail authorities had never had to deal with a group of hikers of this size before, and before the particulars of the event were hammered out, the Dutch bankers arrived in 17 buses plus refreshment vehicles.

Dave and I had encountered numerous signs during our trek instructing us to walk side by side. This pushed us from the grassless portion of the trail, to the frequently drenched edges—the natural tendency was to walk single file on the drier and barren middle part of the Path. Walking single file, unfortunately, has the effect of narrowing the pinch points, causing irreversible damage to the ground and any uncovered artifacts of the Roman period that might lie beneath it. While the exposed masonry is the most eye-catching portion of the Wall, the adjacent turf, which was used for access and for defensive berms and earthworks, is likewise archaeologically invaluable.[36]

The Dutch bankers walked single file, and in silence—they were instructed to remain quiet, perhaps as a way of demonstrating reverence. The resulting damage to the Path, in the form of trampled ground that later caused erosion, created a massive controversy amongst both historians and conservationists, many of whom had been opposed to the idea of a public access trail from the outset.

AMRO Bank planned a similar event in September 2006 with 1,400 bankers when the ground was much less waterlogged. Communication between event organizers and trail authorities was also greatly improved. This time, the throngs of hikers were spread out among four different points along the Path, and the damage that ensued was not nearly as extensive. The Path has since been rerouted so that it no longer passes directly by Milecastle 38 in order to prevent further harm.

Small sections of the Wall have suffered damage (and even a section of Wall near Steel Rigg collapsed) in recent years due to hikers climbing on top for "selfies." The Romans left behind many hidden treasures, including over 13,000 coins left behind in a cache in Carawburgh. Clandestine digging by "night hawkers" armed with metal detectors looking for Roman artifacts such as coins, buttons, and other valuable objects, have resulted in damaging turf digging in areas close to the Wall. Several thieves have been caught and prosecuted by the authorities.[37]

The overall amount of archaeological finds at or near the Wall continues to stun both professional and amateur diggers alike. Recently, in a dig at Vindolanda near the Wall, a 5th-century chalice covered in Christian iconography was discovered.[38] Other invaluable finds from Vindolanda include wooden writing tablets that soldiers used as letters, describing their daily routines, concerns, and "wish lists" for goods they hoped to have shipped to them.

Many of the tablets have been perfectly preserved in the waterlogged and anaerobic earth since being discarded by the Romans and remain legible. One of these, which was scripted by a cavalry officer, a Decurion named Masculus included an appeal to his commander to send reinforcements of beer. In a message to Prefect Cerialis he wrote, "I ask you to order beer, which the soldiers don't have, to be sent." Archaeologists have also found evidence of beer barrels, which they estimated would have had capacities of up to 300 gallons, indicating that the presence of a substantial brewery at the site.[39] It amused me to think that although divided by two millennia, both the Romans and we shared a common requirement for "heart-starters."

The discovery at Vindolanda in 2019 of an ancient gridded gaming board points to the basic requirement of Romans to fill hours of mundane downtime between bouts of military duty. Archaeologists who excavated a 3rd-century CE bathhouse at Vindolanda discovered the game. The grid on the stone board is for a game called "ludus latrunculorum" ("the game of mercenaries"), a game first mentioned in the 2nd century BCE by the writer Varro. A poem by an anonymous writer from the 1st century CE observed that opposing players captured each other's pieces by moving backwards and forwards on the board, like a prototypical version of modern-day checkers.[40]

Archaeologists in recent years have also found numerous

examples of Roman graffiti on the Wall, including phallus etchings. Rather than an attempt at ribald humor, the crude depictions of male genitalia were considered good luck charms.

Foot traffic overall appeared to be rather light along the Path. We usually encountered no more than three to four hikers a day during our walks—certainly nothing like the heavily hiked Appalachian Trail, when I would meet up to 40–50 fellow hikers per day. This, and the lack of camping along the Path, did not lead to the camaraderie—such as hikers constantly exchanging information about weather, upcoming climbs, and other vagaries of the Path—borne of a shared experience such as that found on the American wilderness trails.

We were hiking over the geological formation named the Whin Sill, which features dolerite outcrops across Cumbria and Northumberland, extending to the famous North Sea island of Lindisfarne. Dolerite is an extremely dense igneous rock, and the Romans could not shape it for Wall stones, opting instead to use nearby and much more malleable blocks of limestone and sandstone. The rolling, treeless and grassless ridge of the Whin Sill, flecked with ancient ruins, reminded me of Tolkien's depictions of the Weather Hills in *The Lord of the Rings*.

The impenetrable fog rising from the ground prevented us from seeing one of the more picturesque views along the Wall, the sapphire blue ice age loughs scattered to the north, often referred to as Northumberland's version of the Lake District.

Much like my earlier hikes on the Appalachian Trail, the rain had become a constant feature, and with a slate gray dome surrounding us, there was no prospect for a dry and sunny deliverance anytime soon. When discomfort becomes the norm, it is no longer as irksome, and the thought of the ultimate reward of a hot shower and dry clothes made my fleeting misery somewhat more manageable

We walked in silence for the most part. The roller coaster sequence of rocky hills was requiring more exertion, and with it, a shortness of breath that minimized conversation. I had descended one particularly challenging hill and had crossed a short gap and made my way up the next one when I looked back down. Dave, who was now behind me, had just started his ascent. When I glanced down, I spotted the famous sycamore tree between the two hills and realized that we had just walked by Sycamore Gap. This is perhaps the most iconic and photographed point on the Path, made famous by the film *Robin Hood: Prince of Thieves*, featuring Kevin Costner, Alan Rickman and Morgan Freeman. It is such a well-known landmark that a local brewer chose Sycamore Gap as the name for its pale ale, and it would be among the selections of beer available at the pub we visited that evening.

I shouted out my discovery to a wheezing Dave, who was exhausted by this point and thoroughly unimpressed by my sighting: "I don't care, if you've seen one sycamore tree then you've seen bloody all of them," he huffed. Despite his later admission that the tree deserved a considerably less dismissive appraisal, he had a point, I inwardly admitted, as I turned and headed back up the Path.

That was my Philistine moment. Sometimes the scenic opportunity arrives at precisely the wrong time. The guidebooks and Hadrian's Wall Instagram account, which we frequently consulted, have countless impressive photographs of Sycamore Gap, so it was remiss of me to peremptorily dismiss it. In fact, I was so single-mindedly marching along the trail that I missed the landmark altogether and when Mark pointed it out to me, turning back did not feel like a viable option. My conscience momentarily told me that I should have stopped and paused to admire it, but a combination of the pounding rain and my aching body won the argument and I hardly broke step in pushing on up the next slope, presumably in the vague direction of our ultimate destination. Mark, to his credit, found my uber-truculence mildly amusing—probably having witnessed it on a few occasions before. The siren's call of the day's "heart-starter" in a North Country pub accompanied by a gigantic dinner trumped all thoughts of admiring the scenery. On a sunny day I may have felt differently about it, but appreciation of the Path's bucolic charms was, to my loss, far outranked by the lure of dry clothes and a warm room. I also managed to convince myself that I couldn't be the only denier of famous monument or natural beauty in history, and that a person's immediate appreciation of the qualities such objects on offer can be thwarted by external factors such as the weather or whether a good book at home might be more alluring than a pair of soaked and aching legs. In a similar vein, maybe there have been visitors to the Colosseum in Rome who on burningly hot days irritatedly concluded that this wonder could do with a bit of restorative masonry, or others who when standing in a biblical downpour at Stonehenge might have preferred to see the stones which were lying on the ground to instead be arranged upright in a pleasingly circular formation. Context and timing are everything—or so I was prepared to self-righteously believe as I slogged through the inclement weather, which was assailing the Northumbrian uplands, towards our ultimate sanctuary otherwise known as Vallum Lodge.

By this time, we could spot the village of Twice Brewed, a small clutch of buildings in a valley to our left, bisected by the Military Road. We had one more major obstacle to overcome before we hiked down to Once Brewed—the climb down Peel Crags, via its rain-soaked western extremity, Cat Stairs.

I very gingerly approached the steps leading down the western side of Peel Crags and peered down the Cat Stairs. From my view at the top, it resembled the backside of a brontosaurus—a massive hump that dipped at a steep sixty-degree angle for about one hundred feet before reaching the safety of Peel Gap.

A young American couple was also at the edge studying the descent, and I invited them to go ahead of me. "Why," the woman asked, "do you want us to cushion you when you roll downhill?" She had a point—there was no rail or any type of jutting rocks that would substitute as hand rungs. One misstep on a rain slickened rock and I would instantly transform myself into a hapless Warner Brothers cartoon character taking a bone-crushing slide down to the bottom.

I somehow made it down without incurring any physical or psychological damage, and looked back up at Dave, who was perhaps even more circumspect than I was as he navigated the descent at a snail's pace.

There was a moment as we approached Cat Stairs where the terrain below was not visible, and it felt like we were about to step off the edge of a cliff. My mood had not lightened since my cursory dismissal of Sycamore Gap and looking ahead to Cat Stairs and the optical illusion of a sheer drop, which it presented at that very point, intensified my exasperation. Hours of persistent downpours can do strange things to one's equanimity and my mind, never being far away from revisiting an old favorite song or film, managed to conjure up both media forms at the precise moment. Alongside scrolling back to an old favorite song of mine from my university days in "You Disappear from View" by The Teardrop Explodes, I revisited the "Leap of Faith" scene in Indiana Jones and the Last Crusade *where Indy is forced to cross a chasm on invisible stones. Less mystically, the supercharged fury of John McEnroe yelling, "you cannot be serious!" at a Wimbledon tennis referee also came to mind. This quickly segued into a sense of irate disbelief that the publishers of our Hadrian's Wall guides could have missed this "juncture of infinity," which on reflection I wish I had photographed for posterity and proof that I had not completely lost the plot. What were we expected to do—climb down, scramble down, cross our fingers and hope for the best, or even do what Indy did and throw some pebbles in the hope that they might mark the invisible path to safety? Or would this be the moment when the seductive siren's call of restorative drinks at the Twice Brewed Inn would lure me over the edge to be dashed upon the rocks below? Whilst catastrophizing my way through an array of worst-case scenarios, my sense of humor and more pertinently my faith in the safety of the Path momentarily left me and I silently cursed myself for not opting for the flat land detour that ran through a field of unthreatening sheep next to the outcropping. My preference for dry weather hiking was cemented as the path to safety, although still treacherous in the wet conditions, hove into view as I approached the "point of no return" and contrary to my expectations I completed my descent without injury. I realized then*

Cat Stairs (Mark Clegg).

that there is no escape from the bad weather on a hike and that it can play tricks on you if you experience too much of it. If I were to hike the Path again I would definitely take it on in shorter sections than our compressed itinerary had compelled us to do.

After reconnecting at Peel Gap, we breathed deep sighs of relief and agreed that some sort of handrail should be added to Cat Stairs, even if that risked slightly disturbing the natural features of the crag.

We had a short descent ahead of us as we hiked down the Whin Sill ridge into the hamlet of Once Brewed or Twice Brewed, depending on which entrance you take into the tiny town. Those entering from the east are greeted with a road sign that welcomes them to Once Brewed; those driving in from the west are notified that they have reached Twice Brewed. The head-scratching etymology stems from a legend during the invasion by the Bonnie Prince Charlie. The British Army commander was apparently unimpressed with the quality of the local ale and ordered his beer to be brewed again.[41]

After reaching the Military Road, we took the wrong turn towards Vallum Lodge, our destination for the evening. We hiked perhaps a quarter mile in the wrong direction before turning around and slogging past speeding cars spraying water at us from the ubiquitous rain puddles that had formed on the road.

Samantha, the vivacious owner of the Vallum Lodge bed and breakfast, greeted us at the door. She offered to wash and dry our rain drenched clothes and directed me to my accommodations—a "snug" which was a small two room cottage adjacent to the lodge that featured a small living area and kitchenette that led to the bedroom. I was pleased to see that the always-reliable Sherpas had dropped off my suitcase in the living area of the snug. I decided to go through my small hiking backpack to take inventory of the water damage—my guidebook, map, and even my passport enclosed in a plastic baggie were all soaked. After the day's events, I reacted to this latest negative development with a sangfroid that I was able to summon up only through the cumulative experience of dealing with the ups and downs of thousands of miles of hiking over more than four decades. It was, I knew, all going to be okay.

I took a long shower, put on dry clothes and relaxed on the bed, staring at the ceiling. I thought of my hikes on the AT and how much I enjoyed this part of the day when the hard work was behind me, and I unwound inside my tent while reading a paperback before ultimately nodding off. Our timetable that evening to eat dinner in the local pub was tight, so I did not have much time for quiet reflection and headed out to meet Dave, who had texted me with the happy news that Samantha would be giving us a lift. I was at the door to my snug as Samantha and Dave waited for me inside her black Mercedes S-Class in the driving rain. Of course, I struggled mightily with the keys and lock until Dave walked out of the car and locked it for me.

Our stay at Vallum Lodge was a real morale-booster. It was warm

---

Mark's "snug" (Mark Clegg)

and inviting and Samantha, who said that she frequently hiked the Path, was clearly attuned to how bad weather hiking can crush the spirits of even the most hardened travellers. She offered to dry our waterlogged clothes on the Aga stove and showed me to my room, which to my delight boasted a foot spa. I have to admit to a smidgeon of envy at Mark being allocated the "snug" but this soon dissipated as I settled into the comfort of my room and began to thaw out. I drank, or more accurately inhaled, the coffee and biscuits provided, nailed a few work emails and began to feel a little more human again. Thoughts inevitably turned towards heart-starters and the cuisine on offer at the adjacent (and only) hostelry.

Despite having walked in the region of 17 miles across hilly terrain with often treacherous (and at Cat Stairs, invisible) underfoot conditions, the potentially most risky walking of the day would be to the pub given the bad weather, absence of sidewalks and minimal street lighting, added to which was the high speeds at which cars would pass through the village. Anticipating this, Samantha drove us the short 200-yard distance to Twice Brewed, the sprawling pub where we would be eating our dinner. The dining choices in town were obviously limited, which meant that Twice Brewed was crawling with hikers all in search of a restorative pint and warm meal.

As was often the case after a long and wet hike, I was not famished and picked slowly at my forgettable meal of chicken and roasted potatoes. Dave was in a relaxed frame of mind and outlined the tentative plans for his oldest daughter's wedding in Scotland scheduled for the spring of 2021. It was still early days, with the logistics and wedding administration (or "wedmin" as his daughter Kirsty had christened it) still to be determined with the exception of the choice of venue and an agreement that the males amongst the wedding party would not be wearing kilts.

His son Calum divided his time between studying Spanish and French at the University of Southampton and playing lead guitar and songwriting for his "metalcore" band named Defences, which had recently completed a mini-tour of the UK, including a gig at Newcastle's iconic "Think Tank" venue, and a homecoming performance at London's Camden Underworld. While in Dave's estimation the latter probably only made the band a few hundred dollars at most, he felt that the enthusiastic response of the audience meant so much to Calum and his band and enabled them to finish the tour on a high note. Much to Dave's amusement, Calum at the time was a supporter of Jeremy Corbyn and the Labour Party, reflecting Dave's own intense but short-lived dalliance with left wing politics as a teenager in the 1970s. Calum had already admitted concerns that his political affiliations may follow a similar shifting pattern to Dave's with the passing of time in speculating that he would follow the famous adage loosely attributed to Winston Churchill—"at the age of 20 you vote with your heart, but at 40 you're more likely to vote with your head." Corbyn was perhaps the most left-leaning leader of Labour in the past half-century, and the early polls, which would be borne out by the subsequent election in December, pointed to a decisive win for Johnson and the Conservative Party. That election would eliminate any remaining hope for those committed to stopping Brexit.

Dave would be returning to the north of England in a few weeks to take his third and youngest child, Aimee, to visit the university in Durham with a view to studying music. Dave's admission that despite a profound love of music he was "unable to play a note," and that this has long since led him to the conclusion that his children's musical prowess must have emanated from his wife's side.

The conversation took a more lively turn when we began reminiscing about our time together in London 25 years ago. The wild banking culture in London was quite the opposite of the rather staid environment I was more accustomed to in the United States. Extended beer or wine-soaked lunches that lasted into the mid-afternoon were the norm, and office gatherings in the evenings at pubs or wine bars were raucous affairs that could only be patched together later by the combined hazy memories of the participants.

My introduction to London drinking culture was at a wine bar called Balls Brothers close to my office in Southwark, located on the south side of London Bridge. My near empty or even half-filled glass of Australian Sunny Cliff chardonnay would, without any prompting on my part, repeatedly be refilled by an ebullient colleague. My last memory of that particular evening involved being locked on the floor in a rugby scrum with several associates while the barman good-naturedly smiled and shook his head.

I remembered crossing London Bridge on many mornings on my way to work trying to avoid the vomit slicks left behind by the previous evening's late-night revelers. The memories of Christmas parties came flooding back, and I recalled a colleague who passed out on a stack of coats left in the corner while the head of our credit department got "legless" and had to be poured into the back seat of a cab. Others, emboldened with liquid courage, would gather furtively in the shadows for a quick "snog."

Early on Christmas Eve, a drinks cart would be rolled out at the office, and we would enjoy cocktails until midday. On my way home, I would stop at Leadenhall Market across the Thames River and pick up a pre-ordered turkey, pheasant or goose for Christmas dinner.

There were rollicking "wet the baby's head" bashes celebrating the birth of a child and "leaving parties" for those moving on to a new employer. Much like Medieval Europe and its frequency of religious festivals, London always offered up an event that provided an excuse for a drink.

During my first year or so in London, Dave had educated me on the vagaries of the FA Cup in football (soccer), the intricacies of five-day Test Matches in cricket (which, he insisted, could sometimes end in a highly-entertaining draw), and the differences between the organized mayhem of rugby union and American football. Over countless beers, he shared his knowledge of English music, television, politics, and culture. We shared an off-beat sense of humor, and Dave introduced me to Viz Comics, the irreverent Newcastle-based monthly comic that celebrated such vulgar Geordie anti-heroes as Sid the Sexist, the Fat Slags, and Johnny Fartpants which by then had national popularity. Dave told me that the high point of his experience as a student journalist at Loughborough University was having conducted one of the first interviews of Viz and receiving a humorous and complimentary written response from them. After that "career zenith" he realized that the only trajectory in journalism would be downhill and shifted his focus to the world of finance.

One of my abiding memories of Dave was on a U.S. beach vacation during a rainy day when he was somehow cast into the unlikely position of babysitter for a group of six young children. Amidst the chaos, Dave sat in a lounge chair, intently reading a Martin Amis paperback. His phlegmatic observation at the time was that the room was in perfect equilibrium, with the children transfixed by Robin Williams in *Jumanji* on the TV while he luxuriated in the La-Z-Boy armchair maintaining a "conscientiously aloof view of the proceedings."

We shared an intense interest, bordering on fanaticism, on all matters related to the iconic German techno rock group, Kraftwerk, and traded tips on books and movies. Dave had an interest in my experience with the Athens music scene—I was lucky enough to attend The University of Georgia in the late 1970s to early 1980s when such alternative rock groups as The B-52's, REM, Pylon and Love Tractor were beginning to explode in popularity.

In addition to his inexhaustible knowledge of British culture, which he freely dispensed, I enjoyed Dave's classic English attitude of ironic detachment. This was a particularly valuable defense mechanism at work, where we reported to a well meaning but painfully earnest Canadian named Skip. We were also in a business unit that was slowly sliding into irrelevancy as our employer opted for a change in corporate direction to pursue the elusive lucre of investment banking, at the expense of the plodding but steady profits earned from our traditional lending unit.

With a full head of hair, I was the outlier in what was called the "Chrome Zone," a stretch of cubicles that consisted of four different follicly-challenged middle aged men from all corners of the English-speaking world. As a proud member of the "Chrome Zone Four" Dave had pre-emptively given that appellation to that section of the office. Some years later after he had left banking to join an investment firm he emailed me to report a strange sense of déjà vu upon returning to the bank, now as a customer. After an initial feeling of disorientation caused by a repositioning of partition walls during the intervening years, he realized that the meeting he was attending was being held on the site of the "Chrome Zone."

Our wives got along well, and my daughter was born in London, sandwiched between Dave's first two children, who were born two years apart. Our active friendship continued for more than a decade after I left London in 1996, and we visited with each other's families both in the U.S. and in England. After the Great Recession arrived in 2008, our friendship entered a period of dormancy until I contacted Dave in early 2019 with the idea of hiking Hadrian's Wall.

Mark and I immediately hit it off when he arrived in London and it was great fun to work with him.

Unlike some staff members who came to London from North America, he clearly had a voracious appetite for learning more about UK culture, sport, and music. As a "statto" on sport and music trivia I was delighted to find a willing outlet for my seemingly bottomless reservoir of facts on these subjects. I also enjoyed his sense of humor and turn of phrase that could, for example, completely encapsulate ludicrous or pointless behavior. This happened when he recounted an incidence of a particularly self-important team member being outraged by a colleague "pulling a switcheroo" by exchanging their name cards at a dinner in order to strategically position himself next to a high-ranking visitor from Toronto. This kind of office politicking has always been anathema to me and in my view was endemic of the malaise at the bank at that time. As a founder member of the Chrome Zone I feel entitled to recall that particular episode as being akin to two bald men fighting over a comb.

Mark and I, as committed "have a go" sportsters, also tried out each other's popular national games. We arranged a cricket match against another bank and I was very keen that we should show Mark the full cricket experience. I can still picture him in athletics gear awaiting the first ball, positioned in a baseball stance with his cap reversed whilst the rest of the assembled players were donning our full cricket "whites" including sweaters, floppy wide-brimmed hats and pressed long pants. After a bit of corrective coaching I was pleased to see Mark score his first competitive "run" on English soil. After we successfully saw off the opposition we introduced Mark to the traditional post-match party, which emphasized that cricket, for all of its often-sedentary nature, is a singularly thirst-inducing sport.

For my part, I had my initial exposure to Northern American sport via a softball match when we took on another Canadian bank in London's Regents Park. It was a beautiful, balmy London evening and as we approached the softball pitch, with the "diamond" marked out accurately by the park management, I realized that I did not have the remotest idea of how to play the game. My realization of my status as a softball ingénue magnified as my mind harked back to a holiday that my wife and I had spent with my father-in-law in British Columbia a few years hitherto. I was thrilled at the prospect of visiting a softball batting cage on Victoria Island where a mechanical pitcher projected the ball at slow, medium or fast speeds according to one's preference. Seeking clarification from the operator as to where I should stand, he instructed me to "step up to the plate." Like a number of items of North American sporting jargon such as "the whole nine yards" and "swinging for the bleachers," it's an expression, which has assumed common parlance in UK business-speak without its adopters always understanding the precise meaning. I was no different that morning in British Columbia when, having instructed the operator of the pitching service to set the speed to fast, I stepped onto the plate, confidently assuming that I had correctly understood his instructions. The first ball came at me horizontally and at high speed and I reacted as I would in a cricket game where it's quite normal to face head high "bouncers." I spun around and managed to hit the ball to left field for a short distance but was somewhat confused to see the operator wildly gesticulating towards me from the opposite side of the park. I couldn't hear him and continued to attempt to deflect away the balls that were trained directly on my batting helmet. I was rescued from almost certain injury by my wife who realized what was going on and told me that if I had any aspirations to remain conscious and make it back to the Canadian mainland, it would be advisable for me to desist from standing on the plate.

As I turned from this memory of the British Columbia batting cage, and I commenced with attempting to bluff my way through the Regents Park all-Canadian "battle of the banks" my lack of comprehension of and intimacy with the great game of softball was soon exposed. Standing at first base on, as opposed to next to the base marker, I was quietly getting my head in the game whilst our Canadian opponents, some of whom were lumberjack-sized physical specimens, were becoming progressively more incandescent at my ignorance of softball rules and protocol. One of them complained to the umpire, a mild-mannered soul who clearly had no desire to address the issue with me and request that I should take a couple of steps away from the base. The inevitable conflict soon came to pass as one of the Redwood-sized Canadians hit the ball towards me at first base. Feeling entitled to run through the base he knocked me over, and we got into a tangle of legs in the process. By this time I was prone on the ground and did what I thought was the obvious and only play—to throw the ball backwards and over my head to second base. My opponent was run out and clearly outraged at what, from must have been an unprecedented and in his mind, illegal dismissal. Having played rugby union at school, our collision felt not unusual for a sporting confrontation, and the delighted response of my North American teammates left me satisfied that I had not transgressed. In this instance, the fact that I was oblivious to the rules of softball had worked to my team's advantage. I don't recall how the game finished but I do recall that the settling of our differences was assisted by copious amounts of Molson beer, which had been kindly donated by the event's sponsor.

Following Mark's return to the U.S., we kept in touch and on various Transatlantic visits I was able to join him at baseball games at the Atlanta Braves and Houston Astros stadiums and visiting local tourist haunts such as Stone Mountain and the Johnson Space Center. I was very taken by our visit to Turner Field to watch the Atlanta Braves. It was my first live exposure to Major League Baseball and concluded that I would have loved to have the opportunity to play baseball in the UK. The slickness of the stadium hospitality was in a different league to anything I had experienced elsewhere—the process of having your food and drink brought to your seat by a server with a hand-held terminal might be commonplace in the U.S., but not in the UK. Even now, in major UK sporting stadia you can find yourself having to negotiate entry to a badly organized queue without offending someone who may or may not have joined it before you, or even worse be sucked involuntarily into a human melee in trying to get half-time refreshments. I liked Atlanta and particularly took to the southern cuisine. Amongst other things, Mark introduced me to the delights of the "low country boil" and after I first experienced blackened catfish I was hooked. I spent an excellent gastronomic weekend in Georgia before moving on to a three-week management course at the Kellogg Institute in Chicago. The food contrast could not have been more stark as I attempted to adapt from hearty wholesome Southern cooking to something called a "wellness plate" served up my bank's management course, which was encouraging us to eat healthily, but appeared to be a carefully arranged selection of salad and minimal protein. The sight of it made me feel faint with hunger and at any opportunity I ventured into Chicago in search of sustenance. I knew that there were some aspects of the UK which Mark missed and thus on my visits to his home in Atlanta, I would always arrive with a welcome pack consisting of the anarchically funny Viz Comics, Trebor Extra Strong Mints, and Bassett's Wine Gums. A few years later when Mark moved to Texas, we hatched a plan for my son and I to travel there to experience a rodeo. This trip never materialized as I contrived to break my arm while playing cricket and was unable to travel. I have lost count of the number of times that people have asked me with bemused expressions as to how I could manage to break—and not a modest break—but a clean seven-centimeter spiral break of my humerus bone playing in the outfield in such an ostensibly low-impact recreational occupation as village green cricket. My son described me as a "weekend warrior"—a middle-aged man who is a danger to himself in trying to play like a 20-year-old with a competitive mania that was guaranteed to eventuate in self-harm. I once even managed to break my rib simply by challenging my son to a 50-metre sprint (yes, I should have jogged) from my car to the front door of our local swimming pool by somehow failing to manage the seemingly failsafe exercise of touching the ground with my feet at every step. I felt like Wile E. Coyote scurrying off the cliff edge and with an air of blank resignation holding up the "That's all Folks" placard as my legs spun in slapstick suspension in mid-air before I crashed chest-first onto the path, whilst quizzical parents also on their way to the swimming class must have wondered if they had ever witnessed anything quite so klutz-like. The general humour, which was always a part of our interactions continued via email. Sometimes an isolated jest can be invaluable in easing the stress of an arduous day and I remember being amused by several of his observations. One such referred to the impending merger in 2001 of his employer, Wachovia Bank, and First Union, with Mark suggesting that it would be apt to rename the combined entity "Fuchovia." The email contact could also be invaluable when I needed something of a morale booster. On reading the news of David Bowie's death on that miserable day in early January 2016, I knew that Mark, although we had not been in recent contact, would be one person with whom I could share my shock and sadness and reminisce over favorite songs and live performances. It seems strange to think of it now, but as I sat in an empty office very early that morning before anyone else had arrived, I felt disorientated and upset at the news. A good friend is someone who is there both when you need them and knows why you need them.

Dave's characterization of my one forgettable encounter with cricket was spot on. My approach to bowling was to throw a baseball type fastball using a ten-meter running head start. Of course, the proper way to bowl is to use a windmill style motion with a "twelve o'clock" release point and bounce the ball in front of the batter and the wicket. Instead, I threw high velocity pitches that flew by the batsman at waist level—these pitches/bowls would have been perfect strikes in baseball, but illegal and unheard of in cricket. The elderly batsman was literally shaking as he awaited my delivery. In fairness to him, the last thing he had expected for his outing was a wild American bowling like someone at a carnival trying to knock over a stack of milk bottles in hopes of winning a stuffed animal prize for his girlfriend.

Our opponents, who had arranged the outing, had a good sense of humor and named me "Man of the Match," that included a mock ceremony and the presentation of a bottle of champagne.

Dave and I later enjoyed an outing at Lord's, the iconic

"Cathedral" of English Cricket. Unfortunately, the South African team dispatched the English side early and with ease, leading to one inebriated "Saffer" exclaiming to the despondent, departing crowd that his team's victory had resulted in a "sea of happiness."

Even the most one-eyed of English cricket supporters would have felt an element of sympathy for the unbridled elation of the supporters of the South African "Proteas" team that day. As a sporting nation, South Africa had recently re-emerged from forced exile after it had been banned, due to its loathsome Apartheid racial segregation policy, from conducting overseas tours for the previous two decades. Chatting to some of the euphoric South African supporters that day it is no exaggeration to suggest that it felt like an entire nation was being slowly released from the burden of being judged by the rest of the world through the prism of its government's past actions, and, in the case of those present at Lord's, were raucously enjoying once again the simple pleasure of getting behind their team in a sporting environment. And in common with many sporting nations, being able to "put one over" on England on our home territory is quite evidently an exquisite pleasure. I can't imagine why! But Mark's cautionary words of "hubris gets you very time"—when a country's collective sporting ego writes checks that the collective talents of their representative teams cannot always cash—soon came true for our new-found South African "frenemies."

England would get its revenge several weeks later, when bowler Devon Malcolm destroyed the South Africans in a rematch. This happened to occur on the very day that my daughter, Tess, was born in a Westminster hospital. After the celebratory photographs had been made and phone calls to family members back in the United States had been completed, I repaired to the pub across the street. While sipping a couple of pints of bitter and soaking in the fact that I was now a father, I watched on the pub television one of the most incandescent sporting moments that I had every witnessed. Devon Malcolm completed a "9 for 57" bowling performance, which was a rarity in top-flight cricket. For an American audience, it equated roughly to Wilt Chamberlain's 100-point performance in basketball or Don Larsen's "perfect game" pitched in baseball's World Series.

When I called that day to tell Dave that my daughter Tess had been born, the subject switched to that day's cricket test match and Malcolm's legendary performance. Dave, by his own admission, "has never been averse to a harmless piece of sporting '*schadenfreude*'" and mischievously noted, "It looks like the sea of happiness has turned into a swamp of despair."

We settled up on the bill and when we walked outside, were thrilled to discover that there was a brief break in the incessant rain. We walked, in almost total darkness, the 200 meters distance back to Vallum Lodge. I managed to open this door with just the right jiggle of the key, walked in, and collapsed on the bed. I woke up several times during the course of the night to the sound of rain pounding the roof of my "snug."

CHAPTER 4

Cumbria

After returning to Vallum Lodge the previous evening, we had decided not to head into the lounge for a "sundowner." This proved to be a mistake. There was another vocal group of lady hikers from York-shire in the lounge as I passed by towards my room and they were clearly having a blast. On venturing into the lounge the following morning I regretted not having joined them as I saw the high qual-ity of the wines available by the glass at a cheap price. This fuelled my already high opinion of Vallum Lodge, which took a further uptick, as we were able to benefit from some "dog therapy" during breakfast. Samantha's dog Branson endeared himself to us during breakfast and made me think of my Portuguese Water Dog Juno who we frequently took to my kids' universities to provide her own brand of "dog ther-apy" to their stressed-out friendship groups at exam times. At home in London, Juno employs on an ongoing basis the same brazen canine tableside tactics as Branson—and which is probably practiced by dogs in all points of the UK if not globally—of gazing with heart-melting irresistibility at you until you cave in and agree to share or even sacri-fice your breakfast. That kind of suasion never fails with me, anyway.

I woke up the next morning at 10 minutes before 8, still exhausted and feeling vaguely hungover. I had no time for a shower—break-fast was being served promptly at 8, so I put on some dry clothes and walked the short distance to the breakfast room in the main building.

I could barely get down the scrambled eggs and smoked salmon. I was not only aching from the previous day's walk, but I was still feeling strangely chilled. I picked at my food and fervently wished that I could take what is called a "zero day" on the AT—total rest and relaxation, with the only exertion limited to a walk (or two) down to the pub. My sense of dread was further driven by the knowledge that the hike on this day would offer no relief—we had 17 miles to cover on another rainy day before we would arrive in Walton, our destination for the evening.

Branson, the fortunate English Cocker Spaniel who had full access to the lodge, made his rounds from table to table, never begging for food, only looking for a pat on the head or some other form of positive affirmation. Samantha poured us another cup of coffee and mentioned that Branson "is so sad when guests leave in the morning, so happy when new ones arrive in the afternoon."

Cherish them as we do, and for all that we think we are personally indispensable to them, dogs are nothing if not pragmatists.

Dave and I plotted our course for the day. We would climb back up the Whin Sill ridgeline to rejoin the Path and shortly thereafter, cross the highest point along the Wall. We would continue walking along the crest of the Whin Sill for several miles before slowly departing from the moors with a steady descent back down into lush farmland. We would leave Northumberland and cross the county border into Cumbria in the late afternoon, and in all likelihood, would not reach Walton until the early evening.

The ever-gregarious Samantha packed us a couple of sandwiches with potato chips—there would be few opportunities for food along the way, and it is unlikely we would have much time for a sit-down lunch in any event. By this time (despite her being younger than either of us), we were privately referring to Samantha as "mum" due to her warm and soothing nature.

We set out once again with what was now our constant companion, a steady rainfall. We had to retrace about one mile from the previous afternoon to reach Steel Rigg, which would once again put us on top of the Whin Sill. I always felt cheated during my hikes along the AT when I veered off the path and was not accumulating official mileage just to once again reach the "actual Trail"—I had the same feeling this morning, particularly since I dreaded the damp and bone-crunching ordeal that awaited us.

As we made our way back up towards Steel Rigg and the resumption of the Path, I took a photograph of a horse and immediately sent it to my family to indicate that we were off again on the next section. The immediate response from my wife was "why the long face?" a joke that is as old as the hills but which she knows that my family has allowed me to persist in re-using on several occasions. It's fair to say that the joke doesn't travel well as I also tried it out on my colleagues in Munich, Luxembourg and Paris and received indulgently bemused responses across the board. But I am occasionally overtaken by the urge to recount corny, past their sell-by date witticisms, which have a high probability of producing an exasperated roll of the eyes from the unfortunate recipients. Equally with the right audience, the dog-eared, exhausted gag can nonetheless be greeted by a warm reception like the reappearance of a slightly gauche but loyal friend (and accompanied by the occasional drum roll and cymbal crash to round off the experience). Anyway, dreadful joke or not, it enabled me to deflect thoughts from the hard walking in inhospitable conditions which we knew awaited us. After the comfortable and welcoming stay at Vallum Lodge I had a renewed positivity about me and already the scenery was appearing far more attractive than when I had my "cultural outage" the previous day on failing to appreciate Sycamore Gap in all of its majesty.

We were now in the period of our hike where the Wall was largely intact and we were walking through a quite captivatingly beautiful wilderness. Pounding rain can quite quickly put me onto automatic pilot as I frequently had to march quickly ahead to combat the unfriendly elements, but even with that one can only marvel at how the Wall could have been built in the first place. Rather like the creation of Stonehenge in Wiltshire the efforts that must have been made in the construction process during those ancient days seem superhuman and barely credible.

We climbed Steel Rigg in short order and were engulfed in

Mark on Steel Rigg (David Wilmot).

a shroud of mist that limited visibility to a few hundred feet. We walked along the top of the ridge and zigzagged between the remnants of wall and turret ruins and reached Green Slack, the highest point of the Path, which was marked, by a metal trig point, at 1,132 feet.

I recorded a brief video and posted it to our whatsapp account for our families. The responses were immediate, and remarked upon the beauty of the surroundings, a message that I was determined to keep in mind as the weather closed in on us during the day. I certainly wanted to avoid a repeat of the previous day's growing levels of disgruntlement at the persistent rain deluge.

We talked briefly with a hiker headed in the opposite direction, who laughed and rolled her eyes when we told her we were headed to Walton. She and her companion had left Lanercost and were headed to Steel Rigg—about half the 17-mile distance that the always overly ambitious Sherpas had planned for us.

We walked by Milecastle 42, which impossibly had a gate that opened up to a steep, south-facing slope. The Romans were not going to allow daunting terrain or common sense to interfere with a plan developed by someone who likely had no knowledge of the local topography.

Milecastle 43 abutted a rambling modern farm called Great Chesters (not to be confused with Chesters Fort, which we stopped by earlier on our journey). We passed through a 1,200-acre working farm, replete with a massive barn and sheds, just off the ridgeline. The remains of a three-acre Roman fort was situated adjacent to the farmhouse, and it received its water from an aqueduct (constructed by the Romans) connected to the water source six miles distant in the beautifully named Halfwhistle Burn.

Cloud breaks were starting to appear, and I noticed in the distant valleys the first signs of fall, in the form of amber colored leaves appearing on ash and oak trees. The arrival of autumn in England was always a subtle transition, and it does not offer the explosion of colors that I was accustomed to while growing up near the Appalachian Mountains. I remember what the author Bill Bryson had written about landscapes in Britain—they are typically a gentler watercolor "child's book" style of charm, versus the "knock you off your feet" roaring waterfalls and jagged mountains that we consider representative of American natural beauty.

Although it was late September, temperatures were still warm, which surprised me—I had experienced this change of season three times while living in England in the 90s, and I expected a chill in the air, even in the early weeks of fall.

With climate change, storms more associated with weather events in the United States, including intense flooding, have become more prevalent in England. Storm Desmond in late 2015 created by warm air over the Atlantic brought with it record amounts of rainfall, flooding thousands of homes and washing away roads and collapsing bridges in Cumbria. Just three weeks after Desmond, Storm Eva smashed into northern England; once again causing rivers and creeks to overflow their banks and the Cumbrian Lake District town of Glenridding was flooded for the third time in a month, causing millions of dollars in damage and leaving visitors in its local hotel trapped. This quick succession of storms in December 2015 (accompanied by the warmest December on record) created the highest level of rain ever recorded in the UK.[1]

I remembered a recent article that I had read that the carbon impact of my round-trip flight from Atlanta to London would result in something like the equivalent of 260 cubic meters of polar ice melting. Taking responsibility for my "carbon footprint" is something I wrestle with, but not to the extent of foregoing trans–Atlantic travel by plane. This hypocritical and nagging thought stayed with me as the moorlands began to recede and we began our descent once again into verdant farm country.

At some point on every hike, due to fatigue or the focus on the math related to the daily mileage goal, some sections became nothing more than a blur, and this happened on Day Four. We passed ponds, a quarry, winsome hamlets, and a pedestrian traffic light at a railroad crossing near the 12th-century Thirlwall Castle. But I was no longer able to absorb most of the minutiae along the trail. Historical signposts were passed by, unread. I stopped taking photographs of interesting flora and trees and fast disappearing Roman relics. Remnants of the Wall were becoming more and more infrequent as the Path leveled out and we continued to march westward. While swollen grey clouds continued to skid across the sky, the rain held off in the morning, but we knew that our respite was only temporary— weather reports were predicting the return of heavy showers in the afternoon.

I caught up with Dave as we passed a farm just outside the village of Longbyre that had two Quonset-hut shaped "accommodation pods" of a couple of hundred square feet. Both were available, and they were advertised as en-suite, with shower, fridge, and heating.

With hours of hiking still in front of me and with another round of rain fast approaching, the idea of sheltering inside a Hadrian's Wall version of a Microtel held a lot of appeal. But we pushed onward.

The torrential rain had not quite descended upon us yet, but we knew that it was coming for us. When it did come in all of its punitive monotony, I thought back to the Quonset huts and what we would have given for a break in one of those augmented by a bacon sandwich, a hot coffee laced with brandy, and Vallum Lodge–style foot spa—a sort of "Ice Cold in Alex" moment in reverse.

In the mid-afternoon, the Path wound through the town of Gilsland, where we left the county of Northumberland and entered into Cumbria. I could not discern any difference at all when crossing the border, although writer and Hadrian's Wall hiker Hunter Davies noticed a distinct change in accents between Northumberland and Cumbria: "Defenders of the genuine Cumberland dialect, who definitely produce their own dialect poems and booklets and have their regular meetings, consider themselves very different animals from the Northumbrians. The accents become quite different to the ear in only a couple of miles. In the same way, the differences in a few miles from Scotland into England are equally startling to hear."[2]

Dave and I discussed accents, and I admitted I had a difficult time simply distinguishing between a North Country and Scottish pronunciation, and there was no way I would be able to discern any subtle differences between Northumbrian and Cumbrian accents. For instance, Hunter Davies spoke to a Cumbrian who said he had to leave for "a coop of tea and a wesh," which to my untrained ear, sounded like pure Geordie.[3]

Roadwork related detours caused the Path to zigzag through town before opening up again in the countryside, where an extremely well-preserved section of Wall led us on a steady descent down to the River Irthing. The river marked where the original stone wall ended and the turf wall began on the western side of the river. There was an excellent geological reason for this change—Gilsland is situated along the Red Rock Fault, which runs in a north/south direction, where limestone gives way to clay west of the fault line. It is also a watershed—a divide that determines whether streams flow west to the Irish Sea or east to the North Sea.[4] Ultimately, after the Antonine Wall in modern day Scotland was abandoned and Hadrian's Wall was re-commissioned, the stonewall was also extended from the western side of the river to the coast at Bowness-on-Solway, and the Romans achieved their ambitious goal of erecting a coast-to-coast permanent defensive barrier manned by as many as 15,000 soldiers.

The iron footbridge spanning the River Irthing was built in 1984 and had a spare, industrial aesthetic, more reminiscent of our hike through Newcastle, which now seemed like a month ago.

The modern bridge also served as a reminder that nature never rests—the remains of the original Roman bridge that crossed the Irthing were several hundred feet away on dry ground—the churning river had carved an entirely new course over the sweep of two millennia.

After the Path crossed the bridge, it wound its way upward by 200 feet or so to a plateau where the Roman fort of Birdoswald was built. This was one of the few times I felt winded, and took deep breaths: "breathe in roses, blow out candles," was my mantra for negotiating steep climbs. I looked over my shoulder from the crest of the hill to admire the stunning Irthing Valley, which we had just crossed. The path to the top of the plateau was a "switchback" type trail and the view at the summit revealed the sheer drop off from the eastward facing cliff. Once again true to form, the Romans had managed to dig out the Vallum on the southern most extremity of the plateau.

We walked by Birdoswald Fort, one of the few place names along the Path that curiously has an Anglo-Saxon rather than a Roman name origin. The fort, which was manned by Dacian (Romanian) auxiliaries in Roman times, is also an alternative site for the last battle fought by King Arthur (most settings for Arthurian legend are linked to the West Country). The native Britannic tribes that fought the Anglo-Saxon invaders in the north of England after the departure of the Romans in the 5th century CE were referred to by some sources as the "Warriors of Arthur."[5]

After moving past Birdoswald, the rains returned in earnest, and we still had a further six miles to go before reaching Walton, our destination for the evening. If I had spent more time reviewing our itinerary before the trip, I would have asked Sherpas to book us in a hotel in Gilsland. My only solace was the knowledge that this day's extended walk would set us up for an easy 10-mile hike into Carlisle in the morning.

The approach to Walton led us back to the roadway, where we walked along the asphalt surface, and we became the unfortunate unintended targets of cars spraying water as they sped by.

Dave was by now back on the phone with his colleagues, trying to coax a deal through investment committee, so I was forced to rely on the manual directions provided by Sherpas to our bed and break-fast. The monument that would allegedly serve as the landmark for our directions to our lodging was a carved, wooden Roman centurion, which apparently no longer existed; it may have never existed except for in the mind of the guidebook writer—this was not the first time I had been completely flummoxed by English directions, particularly in the age before Google Maps. We walked in circles until I asked a kindly villager for directions, which she cheerfully provided.

The heaviest rain showers that we had experienced on our journey accompanied the final quarter of a mile of our hike for the day. We were admonished by a peloton of bicyclists, who pedaled by and yelled for us to get "on the right side of the road," as a car drove between us. I did not have the energy to offer any resistance and simply ignored the entitled and boorish behavior that is all too prevalent amongst cyclists. Dressing up like harlequins while riding $2,000 bicycles provides a stratospheric boost to the self-importance of far too many cyclists.

It really was not my plan to attempt to participate in an important investment discussion whilst plodding through driving rain along a main road in rapidly darkening conditions. However, it is my good fortune to work with some very smart and pragmatic individuals who did not object to any background interruptions from the weather, livestock, and on this latest occasion, a small peloton of abusive cyclists who had taken umbrage at our walking at the side of the road facing the oncoming traffic. The adverse weather had slowed us down not least through transforming some of the fields that we crossed into bogs; my boots submerging into the quagmire with almost every step. On top of this, I had lost all faith in the accuracy of advised distances to our destinations as indicated in smart phone maps and route map instructions which we had been provided with by Sherpas. I consulted my two sources of measurement, namely my smart phone and my Fitbit watch. By the time we reached our ultimate destination, the smartphone reading showed that we had covered 19.3 miles in total whereas the Fitbit total read 24.3 miles. Whichever metric was closest to reality, it was longer than the anticipated 17 miles and my soaked and aching feet made me feel that the Fitbit had it right.

It had been a tough day's hiking as I was only too keen to tell friends and colleagues after I had returned to London. But my 24.3 Fitbit-miles slog in the rain was put squarely into context recently when a 48-year-old Gloucester man completed the Wallsend to Bowness hike dressed only in a pair of Speedo trunks, a Roman helmet and boots.[6] He decided to do the walk to raise money for the charity Rugby for Heroes and in doing so hit me with the cruel realization that my home city of Gloucester has produced considerably more hardcore hikers than me.

We finally spotted the turnoff to Low Rigg Farm, the 125-acre working farm that also offered bed and breakfast accommodations. The long gravel walkway to the B&B took us by a massive barn, equipment shed, and grain silo. Ms. Ann Thompson, who, along with her husband, Cliff, runs the dairy farm that has been in operation for 30 years, met us at the front door of the massive, two story rectangular limestone structure.

Staying at a working farm was a much-needed salve for my soul. I have dabbled at urban farming for quite some time, with vegetable

Low Rigg Farm (David Wilmot).

and herb gardens and a coop with six hens in my backyard back home. In my early 60s, I still chop and split our firewood. I have long toyed with the idea of spending my retirement years on several acres of land with a small farm.

The ever-efficient Sherpas had dropped off our luggage in the hallway, and Ann directed us to our upstairs bedrooms. After a long shower, I rested on my bed and weighed our options for dinner. The village pub in Walton was another unfortunate victim of the nationwide wave of pub closures, particularly in small towns, that have happened in the last several decades throughout England (although there was one glimmer of hope offered by 2019 statistics, which showed a net gain of 345 pubs).[7] The only alternative was to take a cab to another town that still had a pub, about five miles distant. After conferring with Dave, we decided to spend the night in, sheltered from the weather. We both made do with the sandwiches that our Vallum Lodge "mum" had packed for us earlier that morning. Still chilled from the rain, I threw on an extra blanket before falling into a deep sleep

As we were shown to our rooms, Ann said that she assumed that we were in the market for full English breakfasts the following morning. I told her that I couldn't be more certain of that, particularly as we hadn't eaten since our breakfast with Branson at Vallum Lodge, which by then felt like 100 years before. Having resisted the temptation to eat it en route on our marathon hike that day, I made short work of the sandwich before deciding that with feet still like permafrost, maximizing sleep was without doubt the best policy, in fact the only one.

My early years were spent in Gloucester in England's West Country, where our house was situated right next to Robinswood Hill. My early exposure to living close to an expanse of farmland has given me a permanent affection for farms in the UK. Young as I was, life on the outskirts of Gloucester in the 1960s felt like a rural dreamland and despite being a city-dweller in London for all of my adult life, farm visits have always held a strong allure. At the end of the day's walking, despite feeling like and probably resembling an extra from Moby Dick, *I was pleased that our next port of call was a working farm. I love being at them and arriving at Low Rigg reminded me of a holiday in North Cornwall a few years earlier. On that occasion the kindly owner of Burniere Farm not only allowed me to ride on his recently acquired New Holland CX 720 combine harvester, but also invited me to take the wheel and drive, notwithstanding the risk this posed to his crop yields. I was pathetically grateful at my fulfillment of this boyhood dream, reinforcing my lifelong admiration of anything to do with farming. Being awakened by lowing cattle at Low Rigg the following morning was all part of the welcoming farmyard vibe.*

After awakening to the dawn chorus of this bovine ensemble, I still had a good 90 minutes to wait until the much-awaited arrival of Ann's full English breakfast. This gave me the opportunity to consider what I had discovered so far on our trip. In addition to seeing the Wall and reconnecting with Mark, part of the original motivation was in a way to see what kind of people and places I would encounter in a part of England only 300 miles away from my home but where I would never normally have the opportunity to visit. Villages, farms, guesthouses, and country pubs—I wanted to experience these infrequently visited places and the fact that we were completing the entire journey on foot added to the feeling of something of a journey into the unknown. So as I looked out at the surroundings of the farm I took stock of what I had experienced so far. Very nice people going out of their way to be helpful such as the man we met leaving the pub in Wylam, David, Jerry, Samantha, even the nice lady with the singing dog. All of this was adding a new perspective for me as I began to realize that this kind of holiday, although quite simple in what we were doing—hiking from one side of the country to the other—was quite the opposite of my conventional holidays. It offered a soothing parenthetic relief from the 24/7 Brexit debate in the media which had become an echo chamber of continuous agonizing about a political decision, which had already been reached through a public vote and was not going to be reversed.

The English, more so than even Americans, revere and mythologize their small villages and their timeless features. As Prime Minister John Major famously said in a speech, "Fifty years on from now, Britain will still be the country of long shadows on county [cricket] grounds, warm beer, invincible green suburbs, dog lovers, and—as George Orwell said—old maids bicycling to Holy Communion through the morning mist."[8]

In the early days of World War II, C. Henry Warren sanctified the English village in his appropriately named *England Is a Village*: "England's might is still in her fields and villages, and though the whole weight of mechanized armies rolls over to crush them, in the end they will triumph. The best of England is a village."[9]

Oliver Rackham in his book *The English Landscape* referred to the ancient countryside of Britain as "the England of hamlets and lonely medieval farmsteads, of winding lanes, dark hollow-ways, and intricate footpaths, of thick mixed hedges and many small woods—a land of surprises and still a land of mystery."[10]

Perhaps the most prolific form of British fiction, the murder mystery, typically has an English village as its setting. From Sir Arthur Conan Doyle to Agatha Christie to the modern-day BBC crime dramas (my favorite—*The Midsomer Murders*), the twisting plot with its countless suspects unfolds in a village pub or church cemetery, an ancient country manor or vicarage.

England is slightly more urbanized than the United States, which is to say an overwhelming majority of the nation lives in cities or suburbs—83 percent by 2011 estimates.[11] So there is definitely a feeling of a *Paradise Lost* caused by urbanization as exemplified in the popular national song (and national rugby union anthem, before it was supplanted by "Swing Low") "Jerusalem," originally part of a poem written by William Blake in 1804:

And did the Countenance Divine,
Shine forth upon our clouded hills?

And was Jerusalem builded here
Among these dark Satanic mills? ......

Bring me my Bow *of burning gold:*
Bring me my Arrows of desire:
Bring me my Spear: O clouds unfold:
Bring me my Chariot of fire!

Chapter 4. Cumbria

I will not cease from Mental Fight,
Nor shall my Sword sleep in my hand:
Till we have built Jerusalem,
In Englands green & pleasant Land[12]

William Blake lived in London at the time when a flour mill, employing 6,000 workers, was built near his home, and it was actually referred to in his day as a "Satanic mill." It is easy to imagine that the appearance of massive industrial works in the late 18th century would have been as unsettling as an alien spaceship landing in Times Square in 2020. The mill drove many independent millers out of business, and when it burnt to the ground in 1791, many speculated that those same millers had committed an act of arson.

The hope for redemption through the rediscovery of an idyllic rural past is a theme that resonates to the present day. A second home in England's countryside is the first priority purchase for a London banker or an English film or rock star that has "made it." The Newcastle band Dire Straits ironically included the "in England's green & pleasant land" line in its song "Iron Hand," which described the pitched battle between striking miners and police at the Battle of Orgreave in 1984.

Like all myths, the ones surrounding the English village can be easily punctured. They do not dwell on the bleak job prospects, the destruction of their character by chain stores, or the disappearing heart of villages, the church and the pub. But for the purpose of this trip, I had pushed these concerns to the periphery and immersed myself in the still bountiful charms of the English village.

In the case of Walton, our latest port of call, the best-known native is James Steele, who, despite becoming blind in his youth, became a social reformer, teacher, poet, and musician and wrote a poem celebrating the Wall and his hometown. His writings point to a very positive attitude towards his blindness with the preface to his 1871 anthology Musings in the Dark *in expressing the bold sentiment that "to the writer (Steele), Music and her twin-sister Song, have nobly alleviated the pressure of a great and enduring affliction (his blindness)." A section of his tribute to Walton vividly imagines how the uplifting beauty of its surrounding countryside must have appeared to a sighted person:*

> *"Walton on the Roman Wall!*
> *Fairest village of them all!*
> *Rivers three around thee flow,*
> *Clearest streams man may know!*
> *Irthing, King and Cambeck sally*
> *Sportively to Eden's valley...."*
> *Gazing from thine airy hill,*
> *Far the eye may scan at will*
> *Cliff, and crag, and castled tower,*
> *Sweet St Mary's Vale and bower*
> *Mountains that the landscape crown*
> *Silver firth and stately town,*
> *Scenes that known are loved so long*
> *Fittest themes to grace my song!*
> *"Walton and its crystal springs"*
> *"Founts of wisdom—idle things"*
> *Send in jesting true may be!*
> *They were founts of joy to me!*
> *Hail thy springs and daisied green!*
> *Moor with gorse of golden sheen*
> *Breeze-blown waves of purple heather*
> *Oft I trod in summer weather*
> *Cliff and tower, dale and stream*
> *Hail!–Farewell!—Tis all a dream!*[13]

I agree with Mark that we have to enjoy the here and now and celebrate English village life for what it is. It still delights me when I "discover" a new country village with all of its quaint and unique charms. I've enjoyed them for as long as I can remember, having grown up in a family with extensive roots in the West Country counties of Somerset and Devon. I also tend to agree with Sir John Major that villages will continue as the quiet, beating heart of the English countryside and celebrated as such. I suspect that there will always be TV programs such as The Midsomer Murders *to celebrate them (despite estimates that the body count of perished characters in the fictional villages from that series now totals 221). Port Isaac in Cornwall is another such example, and it has become a significant tourist attraction as a result of its choice as the setting for the* Doc Martin *TV series.*

CHAPTER 5

Carlisle

Brilliant shafts of sunlight beaming through the small gap in the curtains greeted me the next morning. I could hear mooing and whistling outside, and looked through my window to see, on the far side of a four board, post and rail wood fence, a steady line of black and white spotted Holstein-Frisian cattle being led single file out to pasture. I snapped a few photos, pleased by this calm and reassuring introduction to a new day.

After the rain-drenched brutality of the previous day's marathon hike, the morning felt great and positive. A deep sleep had assuaged the hypothermic numbness of the previous evening and waking up to the sound of the lowing cattle made me momentarily feel like I was back in Gloucestershire in my early years delighting in the proximity of farmlands, livestock, and of course my top agricultural draft pick of combine harvesters.

Searching through my iPhone photographs, I came across a newspaper cartoon of a Roman soldier perched in torrential rain on top of the Wall supported only by his shield. He had been lulled to slumber by a kilted Scottish warrior stationed in the ditch below who had used a recital of the day's Scottish soccer results as his soporific assault tactics—"Motherwell 1, Heart of Midlothian 0, East Stirlingshire 0, Hamilton Academicals 0..." and so on. One can almost imagine the somniferous brutality of such aural assault tactics!

With time on my hands before breakfast, the cartoon made me speculate as to how the Romans and the Scots would have played out a 2nd-century CE *version of the famous "Christmas Truce" football match between the warring German and British troops in no-man's-land during the Great War in 1914. How would the game have materialized had the Romans returned their swords to their scabbards and if the Picts had lain down their square head axes and played out a recreational match in honour of Christmas? I conjured up the image of the Romans playing confidently in the style of latter-day "Azzuri" Italian male teams who have won four FIFA World Cups between 1934 and 2006. Although somewhat shunned by modern-day Italian footballers, the key to their early wins was a combination of the hyper-defensive "catenaccio" (door-bolt) system alongside cautious, intelligent, stylish possession football and catching opposing teams on the break with lightning quick raids on goal. Scotland (represented by the Picts in my Hadrian's Wall-side face-off), whilst having produced some of the best individual players to come out of the UK, cannot boast such an august record of footballing achievement in competitions. In my imaginary confrontation the Picts, growing progressively impatient with the Azzurri-style master class, would adopt a somewhat more pragmatic and physical approach, thwarting the Romans with robust tackling and illegal off-the-ball incidents. There follows the inevitable biblical rainfall, reducing the encounter to a sporting lottery of a quagmire-ridden war of attrition and further deteriorating into what the Scots would call a "stramash," a chaotic brawl with numerous sendings-off and a resultant disappointing 0–0 draw before the protagonists shake hands, exchange pleasantries and return to their battle positions. My football-based daydream of a rain-sodden bore-draw with individual virtuosity thwarted by the elements was not entirely detached from reality. One of the quips often made when a "galactico" overseas superstar player comes to England to play in the English Premier League is "yeah he's great but how will he manage playing in Stoke-on-Trent on a soaking wet Tuesday evening against a team whose defence has 'parked the bus' in front of the net (the prosaic English equivalent of the more exotic-sounding Italian catenaccio system referred above)?" The nailed-on certainty of encountering abysmal weather in Scotland and England during the winter will unquestionably have dissuaded a number of such overseas footballing gods from ever taking the plunge of playing in the UK.*

We hadn't eaten much since the previous day's breakfast and I was ready to hoover whatever Ann was kind enough to put in front of us.

Ann prepared us a full breakfast featuring the farm fresh eggs laid by her hens. She used to let them free range, until the badgers and foxes forced them into a coop. I marveled once again at the work that went into delivering a full breakfast fry up, and Ann only had the two of us to serve on that morning.

The sunshine and the relatively short ten-mile distance for our hike restored our spirits, and our improved attitude was further enhanced by the almost completely flat, albeit waterlogged, terrain we covered. The farmland we traversed hugged tree and fence lines, frequently bordered by Dave's beloved discarded farm equipment (I had to admit, the charm of retired tractors standing sentinel over rain-soaked and harvested fields was growing on me). The mud puddles along the Path were too numerous to avoid, so I simply sloshed through them—the adjacent turf was equally drenched from the previous day's rain and offered no better options.

By lunchtime, we had made it to Crosby-on-Eden, a picturesque town located on the banks of its namesake river. While walking along the main street we spotted The Stag's Inn pub, which dates back to the 17th century and had been heavily damaged by the 2015 floods.[1]

We walked through the courtyard and under the low slung, wood beamed medieval ceiling to a table situated next to a window offering a view of the town's high street. We had the place almost to ourselves, and I immediately felt relaxed and at home.

I have always loved village pubs in England—the creaking sounds from the ancient wooden floor planks, the hushed tones of conversation, and the light music that always played in the background, typically playing a song set list as varied as Ethel Merman, early Rolling Stones and Tennessee Ernie Ford. The atmosphere was so calm in the dining and bar area that I could hear the clanking of

---

dishes back in the kitchen, the ring of a distant phone, and the quiet conversation between the two barmaids. Even the light "whoosh" when the barmaid coaxed out our beer from a cask and slowly filled our glasses from the tap relaxed me.

I missed this quiet civility that is so ingrained in the English character—it suffers, like any land, from violence and rowdiness (even a village pub on a Saturday night can be overrun with locals getting "legless"), but it is also still a nation that sprinkles multiple "thank yous" and "pleases" for the simplest requests; where the police are overwhelmingly unarmed and even a stern warning is delivered with politeness.

Everyday discourse is gentler and less edgy in Britain than in America. Honking a car horn, even in the most congested areas of London, happens with much less frequency than in New York or other large American cities. Exceedingly rude behavior is admonished with a simple "that is not on," and the only time I ever saw "the finger" (actually two fingers in Britain—both the middle and index fingers are extended) was between opposing fans at football matches. Invitations to serious conversations to discuss any level of misconduct are offered with a non-threatening "I'd like a word, please" much more soothing than the American version of "Hey, you got a minute?"

I could lose myself for hours in a timeless place like the Stag's Inn pub, but heavy leaden clouds were once again appearing on the horizon, so we did not linger too long over our refreshing pints of John Smith Bitter and Cumberland sausages deliciously lathered with onion gravy.

We navigated our way past puddles, piles of cow droppings and sheep pellets, and bored groups of cattle that were not in the least intimidated by our presence. Dave and I joked that we were in a Pink Floyd album cover competition.

As measured by visible stone, very little of the Wall remained at this point, particularly as we reached the outskirts of Carlisle. I came across what we refer to as "Trail Magic" on the Appalachian Trail—a

Curious cattle near the Path (David Wilmot).

small stand that sold drinks, gum and candy bars on an honor system. I slipped a couple of pound coins into the box and helped myself to a Kit Kat bar and a bottle of water.

While walking along the A689 motorway, we passed a towering horse chestnut tree (a cousin of the American buckeye) next to a driveway that led to a large country estate. As Dave was demonstrating how the English game of "conkers" was played (using horse chestnuts), the owner of the home pulled up in her Porsche and asked us, somewhat suspiciously, if we were looking for anything. Dave was dressed from head to toe in black, including his skullcap. His appearance reminded one of a TV cat burglar—all he needed was a Zorro-style mask to complete his costume—so this might have sparked the owner's concern that we were up to no good.

We passed the old Roman quarry at Bleatarn, which provided further evidence of the ingenuity and industriousness of the

Romans—stone for the Wall was quarried from Bleatarn. After the quarry was fully depleted, the Romans filled it with water and fish and used it as a food source for the nearby garrisoned troops.

The landscape was becoming more estuarial as we slowly inched closer to the sea. We passed rain-swollen rivers, creeks, and canals, their grassy banks almost topped by gray-green rushing water. Bright pink wild pansies and blackberries were scattered in the bushes, and the ivy on the front of the country manors was already changing hues from a lush summer emerald to its rusty autumn burgundy.

Sections of the Path opened up to a flat and featureless horizon, more akin to Holland or Norfolk than northern England. The terrain was becoming distinctly marshier as we made our way westward, ever closer to the sea.

Rain-swollen creek near Carlisle (Mark Clegg).

Because of the 2015 storms, the Path took a detour on our approach in to Carlisle, leading us through Bitt's Park by a wide, paved footpath bordered on both sides by towering oaks. We ambled by a statue of Queen Victoria, past landscaped gardens, and skirted a children's play area.

We climbed up a steep flight of stairs that brought us level with downtown Carlisle, and ventured into the thick pedestrian traffic, made even more dense by the local school that had just released its students.

Carlisle, with a population of c.108,000,[2] is the northernmost city in northwest England before the border with Scotland. Although aware of its rich historical background and interest, I have generally regarded Carlisle as a place that I would quickly pass through or pass by due to its geographic position. As a major rail interchange, I have often changed trains at its Citadel station travelling to or from Scotland, and on our frequent car journeys north of the border we have a 100 percent record of driving past Carlisle rather than stopping by to investigate the city. I would be by no means the only person who through their adult lives could frequently be travelling in the vicinity of Carlisle without ever stopping to explore it. So, on our hike, our arrival gave me the opportunity, albeit transiently, to take a look at Carlisle, the hitherto "overlooked city of the North."

In 2007, Hasbro, the owners of Monopoly, created a Carlisle version of the board game. Carlisle beat off competition from the city of Preston (and popular tourist spots, The Lake District and the Isle of Man) to be nominated as the next northern regional version of the game.[3] Some 10,000 residents voted for the actual Carlisle locations, which were to be displayed on the game board according to the number of votes cast, with Hadrian's Wall occupying the second square. Despite the physical absence of the Wall from Carlisle, with almost all of the stones having either been removed or recycled, and despite the Wall being situated in the "lower rent" section of the board, it clearly retains a significant place in Carlisle's cultural history and self-perception. By contrast, Hasbro also recently introduced the Newcastle version of Monopoly, and the Wall surprisingly did not merit a position on the board.

Carlisle's known history pre-dates even Hadrian's time, with a timber fort believed to have been erected in 72 CE on the site of what was much later to become Carlisle Castle. The Romans called the settlement Luguvalium (meaning "city of Luguwalos," Luguwalos being a masculine Celtic name meaning "strength of Lugus" and referring to Lugus, a deity of the Celtic pantheon).[4] The name was later abbreviated to Luell, and with the prefix Caer became Caer-Luell, and subsequently Carliol and Carlisle.[5]

Subsequent to the departure of the Romans in the 5th century, the Picts laid the city to waste. As England and Scotland emerged as nations, the battles between the two rivals over the sovereignty of the border city of Carlisle occurred over several centuries. Between 1050 and 1745, every English monarch except three either invaded or was invaded by Scotland. Macbeth, the doomed subject of the Shakespeare tragedy, was murdered after losing a battle to the Northumbrians at Dusinane Hill in 1057. In 1307, the English king Edward 1 captured the Scottish border town of Berwick and massacred every man deemed eligible for military service. Centuries more of atrocity and counter atrocity were committed.

These conflicts culminated in the Jacobite rebellion of 1745, when the Pretender Prince Charles Edward, "Bonnie Prince Charlie," marched from Edinburgh and converged upon Carlisle and rode into the city upon a white charger heralded by highland bagpipers. This soon backfired when the Duke of Cumberland bombarded the castle and the Prince's garrison surrendered. The subsequent executions after this and other battles ordered by the Duke earned him the soubriquet "the butcher of Culloden."

The Jacobite occupation of Carlisle Castle was the last time it was attacked and in the early 19th century it was converted into an army barracks, with the Border Regiment being stationed there between 1881 and 1959. Today the castle dominates its surroundings in Carlisle's city centre and is a monument to its violent past, with dungeon walls still displaying the graffiti left behind by unlucky prisoners captured in the endless border conflicts.

Elsewhere in modern-day Carlisle there is plenty of evidence of Roman occupation. The remains of a Roman bath house were uncovered as part of an archaeological dig under the existing pavilion of Carlisle Cricket Club which was in the process of being re-sited due to flood damage.

In addition to several prominent UK figures in the fields of sports, business, media, literature and politics, Carlisle has produced two people who have had an impact upon U.S. politics. These are Edward Tiffin, a U.S. senator and the first governor of Ohio, and Janet Woodrow, mother of Woodrow Wilson, the 28th president of the United States. The President made several visits to Carlisle, most notably on his "pilgrimage of the heart" on 29 December 1918 (just after the end of the Great War), which is commemorated on a plaque on the wall of the Carlisle City Church.

Whilst smaller than Newcastle, Carlisle evidently has the same predilection for partying and the Botchergate area of the town is full of bars and restaurants and gets particularly lively and popular with the students of the University of Cumbria and townsfolk over the weekend.

We weaved in and out of navy blue uniform clad adolescent pupils and walked up the main road towards our destination, a large Victorian guesthouse positioned directly over the site of the original Wall. We were met at the front desk by the proprietor, a thin, bespectacled man who bore a striking resemblance to the rock star Elvis Costello. We later dubbed him Declan McManus (Elvis's actual name), and he mentioned to us several times while we were checking in that he was suffering from a bad head cold.

Sniffling, he led us up the narrow stairway to our rooms. We both faced the busy street, and it was a jolt to once again be bombarded by the noisy street life that was rumbling just below my open window.

All in all, I was very pleased with our accommodations during our walk. While unglamorous, they were well above "bog-standard"—an English expression for very spare or ordinary (similar to "meh" in American English), a characterization more in keeping with the unadorned hostels and motels I stayed in while hiking the Appalachian Trail. I was thankful for the upgrade and the chance to recuperate from the rigors of our daily hikes under more civilized surroundings.

After a brief rest, Dave and I met up at a nearby pub. I managed to stump Dave on an English pop culture trivia question, which was quite an accomplishment. Question: what noted rock group hailed from Carlisle? Answer: Spooky Tooth. Dave has won multiple trivia contests over the years, and I could tell he was disappointed that that bit of arcane knowledge had escaped him. The other bit of Carlisle trivia that I found interesting was the nationalization of the city's pubs, which happened during World War I and was not ended until the 1970s. The reason for this extreme measure was intended to grant governmental authorities the ability to gain greater control over the drinking habits of workers who toiled at the nearby armament factories. Why this step was focused particularly on Carlisle (and kept in place for so long) and not other English cities with munitions works remained a mystery to me.[6]

I cannot disagree with Mark that I was temporarily crushed that he had beaten me on a trivia question, and I can only put it down to the effect of the hard walking and incessantly bad weather that day. If this book were an email I would also have inserted a wink emoji at the end of the preceding sentence!

Although we had another day to go, Carlisle felt like the western "bookend" of our hike and the well-proportioned and modern pub which we found ourselves in could have qualified as one of the anonymous soulless pubs so disliked by the driver of our cab upon arrival in Newcastle on our first day. Notwithstanding that, I was pleased to be back in an urban hostelry watching Premier League football and although still relatively peaceful, with more people in attendance than we had come across in the pubs we had visited over the past five

*days. I had loved the farmlands and wild and beautiful scenery of
the Path, but the familiarity of the urban setting was working a sort
of homing instinct on me and I knew that would only increase as we
spent more time in Carlisle and the end of our pilgrimage approached.*

Over a couple of beers, we planned out our hike for the next
day. We were booked on a 5 p.m. train to London, and we knew that
bus and cabs were hard to find in Bowness-on-Solway, the end of the
Path. The decision was made to catch a cab early the next morning
to Bowness and walk the 14 miles back to Carlisle, where we could
pick up our luggage and still have enough time to hail a cab ride to
the train station. It felt a little odd to leapfrog the final portion of our
walk to hike in a west to east direction, but I was not going to be a
purist—we would still cover the entire distance.

We shoved off from the pub and progressed to our dinner book-
ing at the Spider and Fly, an improbably Gothic themed restaurant
that had received rave local reviews. It was positioned in a bank
of rather attractive-looking shops including a barber shop called
Brazuca 1 Gentry Grooming which was very stylishly furnished with
a photo mural of Johnny Depp as Sweeney Todd. Once in the restaurant, we decided against our table in the main dining area downstairs—it was decorated too much like a dungeon.

Once again, I gave into my hiking-fueled, carnivorous urgings
and ordered a pork belly and black pudding appetizer, followed by a
full serving of haddock and chips. Dave was in an effusive mood, and
he declared that this evening would represent our celebratory dinner.
Although we still had almost a full day and a 14-mile hike ahead of
us, we would be on the train back to London the next evening, hardly
a festive setting for a celebration.

Between frequent refills for my mug of ale and Dave's glass
of claret, we reminisced about our trip and our plans for the next
day. Our waiter came to deliver the check, and we asked about the
weather forecast for the next day. "Rain again, I am afraid," he offered,
with a shrug of the shoulders.

Sensing the approaching end of our adventure, I drank more that evening than whilst we were crossing the more remote stretches of the Path. It was an opportunity to sit back and reflect on the highlights of the week and what it had given us. I also questioned Mark about his experiences hiking the Appalachian Trail and I was impressed by his ability to get through the night sleeping in open air shelters that sounded like they were little more comforting than a normal bus station waiting room. Hearing this, I quickly concluded that there would be little prospect of my being able to take part in any hike with such arduous sleeping conditions. The accommodation and bag forwarding service of the Sherpas had got me through the week and I was so pleased that we were about to complete our coast-to-coast long march. I felt relaxed and was looking forward to a good night's sleep back at the hotel in preparation for the final push the following day. Unfortunately, my mellow feel-good mindset proved to be somewhat premature as there was still an uncomfortable episode in store for me involving a damaged door lock and an ill and extremely disgruntled hotel proprietor. My passage to our ultimate destination of Bowness-on-Solway was not to pass without incident.

CHAPTER 6

Last Leg

Dave texted me early the next morning with the unfortunate news that he was locked out of his room. Upon his return the previous evening, he had turned the key in the deadbolt lock on his door, and the teeth of the lock no longer engaged with the key, leaving him stranded outside in the hallway. He called the main switchboard and with the proprietor *hors de combat*, Dave was relieved to speak to his wife who was extremely helpful. She offered Dave another room, where he slept for the evening, but his luggage was all locked up and would be inaccessible until a locksmith arrived to replace the lock. The irony of the situation was not lost on us—Dave had patiently assisted me with locking and unlocking doors over our journey, but it was he who was the ultimate victim of a broken lock.

This was just a case of bad luck—"accidents will happen," as Elvis Costello once philosophically crooned—and I have to confess to a completely irrational belief that incidents like this always seem to happen when a few "cold drinks" have been taken on board. On another occasion late at night at a drinks party for one of my children's school classes, my mobile phone started ringing and would not cease, causing me immense irritation and a bizarre sense of persecution by an inanimate object. In the event I was fortunate that in the first place that the hotel had a spare room available and secondly that I was able to get through to the hotel proprietor by calling the main switchboard. So at least I was able to get a bed for the night albeit without my laptop and with a mobile phone rapidly running out of charge—the lack of connectivity threw me somewhat. Once again I was reminded at how we so readily build our modus operandi around our smartphones and computers. A few years ago as an experiment, my kids agreed to try to live one day of their life under 1970s-type conditions. Essentially, this "historical experiment" (as I pitched it to them) entailed debarring any use of smartphones and personal computers, and only allowing them to watch terrestrial TV channels. Almost instantaneously they were completely at sea with no social media access with their friends and ability to search on the Internet. Eventually my objective of them opting for the alternative of outdoor pursuits was realized, but not before objecting to me that the whole exercise had been akin to psychological waterboarding—like asking them not to breathe.

This threw a spanner in the works, inasmuch as it would delay the start of our hike by at least an hour, the time estimated before the locksmith would arrive. After we ordered breakfast, Dave asked for an update on the expected arrival of the locksmith, and Declan snorted, "can't you see I have a cold, I am doing the best I can?" When he went back to the kitchen, we had a laugh about this John Cleese-inspired "Basil Fawlty" level of British service, which never hesitated to rudely correct a customer who might be in the wrong.

By this time, I was getting a bit tired of the traditional English breakfast and would have preferred the early version of today's Paleo diet enjoyed by the Roman army, which consisted of wheat pancakes, honey and dates (even though I don't normally care much for dates).

We debated my going ahead and Dave going separately once he gained access to his room. Fortunately, the locksmith arrived early, and he was able to replace the lock in short order. The locksmith was a very jovial, wisecracking North Country character who reassured Dave that this sort of thing happens all the time and that it hadn't resulted from anything that he had done. We had only lost about a half hour to this mini-fiasco, and we hailed a cab for the ride out to Bowness-on-Solway, the start point of the Path for west-to-east hikers.

Our driver mentioned several points of interest along the way, including our first sighting of Scotland, which we could easily make out across the Solway Firth. A common misconception is

Dave overlooking Solway Firth (Mark Clegg).

that Hadrian's Wall straddles the English/Scottish border, but it actually breaks off at a roughly 45-degree angle heading to the north-
east after the Solway Firth, so this was our first sighting of Scotland
over the course of our journey. It was in nearby Carlisle that the Bonnie Prince Charlie and his Highland army invaded England in 1745
and captured that city after a six-day siege (only to be driven out
six weeks later). While few in number, the Highlanders were tradi-
tionally a zealous group of fighters; just three years earlier in 1742, a
Highland force attached to the British Colonial Army had destroyed
an invading Florida based Spanish army in my native Georgia at the
Battle of Bloody Marsh.

   We were dropped off in a thick mist outside the King's Arms, the
pub that marked the official western most point of the Path. There is
a hilarious sequence in the amusing and informative 1974 travel doc-
umentary *The Living Wall* in which the narrator (and author of the

book of the same name), Hunter Davies, interviews local residents in Bowness about the location of the Wall. The responses register on a scale of varying degrees of indifference, from not knowing the Wall existed to believing it ended in another town.[1] Davies regarded the local citizens as furtive and wary, those characteristics imbued in their genetic codes due to centuries of Scottish invasions by land from the north across the Solway Firth and from the west across the sea from Irish pirates.

At one time, Bowness—the name is derived from its geographical location—it is wedged in a bow shaped portion of the ness, or peninsula—was the site of the second largest Roman fort along the Wall, called Maia. The town very much had an "end of the line" feel to it, much like Key West, Florida, or Land's End in Cornwall. Almost any trace of the Romans is now gone, and we were directed by a local to cross the street and hug the coastal line (with the Solway Firth on our left) as we set out. Even in the early 19th century, almost all signs of the Wall had vanished and been used for more utilitarian purposes: "Half the churches, houses, barns, partition-walls, and roads, nay, even down to a very horse-block, were raised out of this Wall. Here the church and village of Boulness (Bowness) had their origin."[2]

The Solway Firth has a rather colorful recent history—it is where the schlock horror classic movie *The Wicker Man*—featuring the incomparable Sir Christopher Lee and the Druidic method of human sacrifice, burning victims alive in a wicker cage—was filmed, and its muddy floor contains the remnants of over 600 uranium depleted tank shells fired by the British Army from the Scottish side of the border.[3] On this day, however, the most harrowing thing springing from the low tide Firth was a stiff wind that brought down a stinging, slanting rain. The shriek of curlews and gulls and oystercatchers accompanied us as we walked along the marsh.

The Scottish border prompted a discussion with Dave, who is married to a Scot, and by his admission, has become an admirer of that land, although he acknowledges it was a slowly developing acquired taste. The two countries maintain a long-standing love-hate

The official start/end of the Path in Bowness (David Wilmot).

relationship, perhaps leaning recently a bit more to the hate side due to Brexit and a resurgent Scottish nationalism. When I lived in London, many of my English friends would mention having a Scottish grandparent or great-grandparent. It seemed, in their minds, to add some intrigue into their bloodlines, in much the same way Americans will boast about some distant connection to a Native American tribe ("my high cheekbones come from my great-grandmother, who was Cherokee").

And so, on to Bowness, the westernmost point of our journey— the coast-to-coast aspect of our hike provided an additional frisson on top of the historical fascination of the Wall itself. Whether going coast-to-coast as we did, or taking a celebrated road route, such as the 2,448-mile-long Chicago–LA Route 66, immortalized in song by numerous artists, the completion of an iconic journey has an undeniable romantic context. Even the A303 highway in England, which runs a comparatively modest 93 miles from Basingstoke in Hampshire to Honiton in Devon via the ancient Stonehenge monument, has a book devoted to it in tribute. So it was a special moment to find myself on the opposite extreme of England to our starting point, albeit the romance of the moment lay definitely in the context of our journey rather than physical surroundings on a bleak September morning. The few local people we saw appeared understandably indifferent to us as yet another pair of transient hikers en route to Carlisle. The initial stretches of our walk back alongside the road towards Carlisle were not particularly user-friendly with a marked absence of sidewalks and a 60-mph speed limit. The grass banks of the road were often quite boggy due to a combination of heavy rainfall and the fact that the area is prone to flooding. Nonetheless, it was a singular, quite special feeling to be there and indulge in some personal reflection. For the past three and a half decades Scotland has played quite a significant part in my adult life and it was a moment to breathe in deeply in a moment of contemplation whilst standing at the end of the Path in England, gazing across the Solway and the steel-grey sky towards the Scots town of Annan and another country. The proximity of Scotland is reflected in several chapters of Solway's cultural history. In 1869 a rail line, the Solway Junction Railway, was opened between Bowness-on-Solway and Annan on the Scottish side of the border. Measuring one mile 176 yards long, the iron girder viaduct was used by Scots, who due to local licensing laws had no access to alcohol on Sundays and used to walk across to the more liberal English side to slake their thirsts.[4] Apparently returning in a less than sober state across the narrow viaduct was fraught with risk but this did little to quell the hedonistic have-thirst-will-travel philosophy of the townspeople of Annan. Historically, the liberalism worked in reverse when it came to weddings. The 1754 Marriage Act outlawed marriage in England under the age of 21 without parental consent, with any breach carrying a sentence of 14 years' transportation (forced deportation to Australia) for the offending clergyman. By contrast, the law

in Scotland permitted anyone over the age of 15 to enter into mar-
riage. Annan's neighboring town of Gretna became renowned as the
elopement centre of the UK for love-struck English youths wishing to
tie the knot. Provided two witnesses were present, virtually anyone
could conduct the ceremony and the local blacksmiths, as respected
members of the local community, were heavily involved in the cottage
betrothal industry, resulting in the coining of the expression "Anvil
priests."[5] *So in theory, teenagers could execute an arbitrage between*
the two legal systems. The "play" would presumably be for a cou-
ple in their late teems to get married by an anvil priest somewhere
in the marriage hotbed on Annan-Gretna, walk the precarious route
across the viaduct to an evening's drinking in the accommodating
"watering-holes" of Bowness-upon-Solway before braving the return
journey to married bliss north of the border.

I was married in Edinburgh on an atypically blisteringly hot
day within sight of its commanding volcanic plug landmark, Arthur's
Seat. Now with my eldest daughter's impending wedding planned for
a venue just outside of Edinburgh, there is an element of our family
history completing a full circle. I love Scotland and its humor—often
self-deprecating, and always razor sharp. One of my first visits there
was to the Borders town of Hawick, and I found evidence of this nat-
ural instinct for finding humor in unlikely places in the names given
to some of the pubs. The first two hostelries I visited had the curious
names of "The Office" and "The Angling Club." On questioning my
hosts as to the origins of these appellations, the consensus of opin-
ion was that they had been given those titles to facilitate being "eco-
nomic with the truth" as to your whereabouts. Hence a person on a
pub-crawl could advance the excuse to their loved one—"Apologies in
advance darling, I'll be delayed at "The Office" this evening." There is
an urban myth that Glasgow and Edinburgh, which sit at either ends
of Scotland's 50-mile "wasp waist," are also poles apart in their predis-
position towards hospitality. The line goes that the Glaswegians are
open and welcoming whereas the citizens of Edinburgh are remote,
privileged and snooty. My wife once told me the gag that the way to tell

the difference between the two cities is that a Glaswegian will tell you, "come on in you'll be having your tea" whereas the modified invitation from a native of Edinburgh would be "come on in you'll have had your tea." All good clean fun and indicative of a country, which doesn't take itself too seriously—sometimes one-liners of this type, can be a useful means of pricking the bubble of any pomposity and regional antipathy. Indeed, Scots comedians have never been averse to promulgating national stereotypes if it will provide an audience with a harmless good laugh. Globally celebrated comedian Billy Connolly once surmised that a combination of the biting cold Scottish climate and the supposed natural aggressiveness of Scots would have unnerved the Roman invaders at the time of the building of the Wall—"they (the Romans) must have hated the climate. If you come from Rome and you wear a wee toga, the Scottish climate isn't everything you would wish for and you'd tend to give it a miss and build a wall instead" and "he (Hadrian) built it because they were probably a bit scared of the Scots. They were probably wandering around Scotland and were set upon by these blue naked people and they must have thought they were on the dark side of the moon and decided that they would stop the empire here, we've got to the edge of civilisation."[6] Another Glaswegian comic, Kevin Bridges, made some hilarious observations on the EU at the time of Scotland's Independence Referendum, stating that an independent Scotland in the EU could have its own currency, the "Smackeroonie" and its own electric plug, a "six-pronger which could double up as an offensive weapon."[7] Just livewire comedy which people who know Glasgow and Scotland—and can relate to the passionate, direct, but always firmly tongue-in-cheek delivery—can share and delight in.

The mischievous Dr. Samuel Johnson referred to oats in his famous Dictionary from 1755 as "a grain which in England is generally given to horses, but in Scotland, supports the people."[8] "Seeing Scotland is only seeing a worse England," is another one of his many famous jabs at his Hibernian neighbors. That attitude resonated with William Hutton, who in 1801 wrote the first modern day journal detailing the coast-to-coast hike of Hadrian's Wall. He wrote, in the prologue to his journal: a Scotsman would consider this (wall) a mighty bulwark a compliment paid to his country; and infer "it was designed to bar a superior power and was the effect of fear, for if two nations could meet upon equal terms there would be no need to raise a wall between them."

A Roman, on the other hand, would reply, "Your country is mountainous, barren, and difficult to conquer. The rough land is your safeguard, not the people; and the inhabitants are so poor they are not worth conquering. On these rests your security."[9]

Quite in contrast to Carlisle, which endured successive occupations by the English and Scots over the centuries, the less populated area along the modern-day western border of England and Scotland was called "the Debatable Lands," and was so lawless during the medieval period that both countries washed their hands of it, declaring by parliamentary decrees that neither would be responsible for governing a remote region overrun by reivers. This created, in essence, an independent anarchic no-go zone ruled by thievery and brute force for three centuries.[10] In 1562, both countries agreed to construct a half-hearted earthen border wall called "Scots Dike" (still visible today) that only extended three and a half miles before either enthusiasm or funds for the project evaporated. The remains of many "bastles" (fortified stone farmsteads) are dotted throughout the border region. These thick walled and sturdily built multi-level structures did not have ground floor doors (there were no stairs, only ladders allowed access to the higher floors) making infiltration by reivers more time-consuming and costly. Stone beacons, one of which still stands in the Cumbrian town of Penrith, were lit to warn the English countryside of imminent Scottish invasions.

Despite the weather conditions, we made great time, covering three miles an hour over the Path on a raised bank that ran parallel to the road we had traveled on from Carlisle. In short order, we passed Port Carlisle, a former canal city and modern-day ghost town, rendered obsolete in the mid–19th century by the introduction of railway. In quick succession we walked past Glasson, Drumburgh, and Easton. One sign posted directions to a town named "Finglan-drigg," the most Norse place name that I had ever seen in England. Northern England is chock full of towns and villages of Viking origin—my surname hearkens back to back to the Norse invaders who settled Yorkshire, so I have always had a soft spot for proper nouns ending in double "g."

Mysteriously, the original Wall (none of which was ever visible on the stretch between Solway and Carlisle) zigzagged 34 times over this flat terrain, which is even more head-scratching when the Romans went to great lengths to maintain linearity in the much more challenging terrain of the Whin Sill.

In Burgh-by-Sands (pronounced "Bruff"), we stepped into St. Michael's Church, where "Edward Longshanks" (King Edward I of England) was laid in state after dying from dysentery when trying to cross the Solway Firth into Scotland to pursue Robert the Bruce of *Braveheart* fame. We were welcomed by a group of local elderly lady volunteers, who handed out cookies and had us sign the guest book. Their funding from the British National Trust depended partly on the amount of tourist traffic the church attracted, and I dropped a few coins in the donation box as I made my way around the small nave of the chapel. The church was built largely from Roman stones pilfered from the Wall, and one stone over the altar featured the visage of a Roman pagan god.[11] The church also included a 14th-century tower called a "yett" which allowed villagers to take refuge during the frequent incursions by Scottish raiders.

We left the church and marched in what was now a downpour. On the village green we also saw a bronze statue, "The Hammer of the Scots," which was built in 2007 to commemorate the 700th anniversary of King Edward I's death. Burgh was also the site of the Roman fort Allabava ("apple orchard"), which was not discovered until 1922. The fort was garrisoned by a multi-national contingent of Moroccans, Frisians, and Ethiopians. The Principia of the fort is believed to be located where St. Michael's Church now stands.

The Path hugged the road and at some chokepoints forced us on the asphalt, where we inevitably caught the full brunt of wet spray from passing cars. My hopes rose in the early afternoon when I spotted a pub in the town of Beaumont (pronounced "Beemont"), but upon closer examination, saw that it was shuttered; another casualty washed up on the shores of English village pub closures.

The Path finally detoured from the road and led us through swampy countryside, and our pace slowed as a result. The River Eden was just to the north of us, on our left, and in certain areas it had flooded into the adjacent farmland that the Path bisected, making it impossible for us to detour around large puddles. My feet were soaked, and I no longer cared; this was, I accepted, simply the natural order of things. "Embrace the suck," as they say on the AT. I had reached the stage of the hike where simply putting one foot forward was no longer dictated by muscle memory; it was only made possible by conscious effort. I was eager to get the last leg behind me, and my rumbling stomach was demanding a serious "grease fix," which would be satisfied by the fish and chips shop (aka "chippy" in Dave-speak) near our hotel which I had passed the previous evening.

Dave was well ahead of me by this point, and on straightaway sections, I could spot him, his phone pressed against his right ear.

This must have been muscle-memory on my part, as the previous evenings "episode of the malfunction door lock" ("lockgate"?) had denied me the opportunity to recharge my phone and we were away from the hotel so quickly the next morning ("hotelxit"?) that my phone was by then running on empty. I didn't mind too much, being permanently connected and available for comment in one's work can be greatly overrated. My younger colleagues find it barely credible that in the 1980s and early 1990s we could have conducted international financing transactions using nothing more sophisticated than telephones, typewriters, and, if you were particularly cutting edge, a fax machine. I'm not convinced that the availability of modern communications media and the obsession with communication to anyone remotely connected with the deal in question via email and social media has saved us any time at all in getting transactions "across the line." And there was nothing like a 36-hour completion meeting (interspersed with "all nighters") to teach one about endurance and the negotiation of legal documents under pressure in transacting financial investments. It also taught me that after a sleepless night working and negotiating, the celebratory drinks the next day generally had a disproportionate impact upon one's sobriety.

As is always the case near the end of an extended hike, I grew reflective—this walk along the Wall was another milestone for me, an accomplishment that would appear silly to many, but something that I had always longed to do. I took a small measure of pride at the physical accomplishment, but I also knew that my body would ache for weeks, and even months, afterwards. My mind began to race forward on what my next hiking adventure might be.... continuing the trek up the AT towards Maine, tackling the Camino Real in Spain, or climbing through Hannibal's path through the Alps? I would weigh my options, and with retirement fast approaching, hopefully have an abundance of time on my hands to plan and research the next walk along history.

I was also comforted by the fact that as awkward as it might seem, it is never too late to seek out an old friend, no matter how distant the last communication might have been. At the time, I took a chance when I reached out to Dave, and I factored in a high likelihood of rejection. It just never hurts to ask.

Farmland gradually gave way to the industrial estates of western Carlisle, and I once again merged with the same group of school children whom we had walked along with the day before. I climbed the long flight of stairs that took me above the river where I was dumped once again on the road of our hotel. As I finished the final steps of the Path, I was disappointed to see that the fish and chips shop had not yet opened. I was starved, and I had had my heart set on some greasy haddock and fries soaked in malt vinegar.

Dave and I hailed a taxi around 4 p.m., in plenty of time to make our train to London, scheduled to leave at 5. We crawled through downtown Carlisle, whose most noticeable feature was a massive Debenhams department store that had been hellscaped into several city blocks and dominated the city centre. It looked like the modernist architecture offspring of a castle that had mated with a public housing estate.

We grabbed a couple of sausage sandwiches in the cozy Gothic domed waiting area of the Victorian train station and slipped into our train right on time. It was Friday, and a lot of folks from the North Country were headed to London for the weekend, it seemed. I sipped on a currant cider that I ordered on a whim that surprisingly hit the spot. I quietly soaked in the sense of accomplishment of completing the 84-mile walk (closer to 100 miles when detours for lodging are added to the total) just weeks before my 61st birthday. I tried not to dwell on the crammed trans–Atlantic flight that my daughter had booked me on for the next morning, or the suffocating 95-degree heat that awaited me when I landed in Atlanta.

I glanced across the waiting room tired, but safe in the knowledge that, as Mark put it, "it (the Path) can't hurt you anymore." I noticed two youngish men both wearing full Manchester United tracksuits and who appeared to be part of the football team's staff, noticeably drinking half pints of lager—perhaps part of the coaching staff rather than the playing staff. Everyone seemed to be gearing up for the weekend in their own way and I was keen to get on the train and settle into debriefing chat and drinks with Mark. I also realized at the time that in keeping with my observations about King's Cross, Victoria, Paddington and Liverpool Street stations having their own associations with destinations and related emotions, Carlisle railway station would now forever be linked in my psyche with the completion of our "conquering" of the Hadrian's Wall Path. It was a very pleasing moment to reflect that we had pulled it off in a very tight timescale, in quite abysmal weather and having had a one-off hiking experience that will remain with me permanently. I was also beginning to quietly realize something that became more apparent in the days that followed—that I had really benefited from the challenge of a demanding daily hike. Whilst my aching muscles constantly admonished me that I was not immediately in the market for a repeat dosage of the 24-mile near-marathon along the lines of our Twice Brewed–Walton leg of the Path, I knew that I would like to do more of it one day and have the opportunity to experience dramatic countryside up close, discover villages and meet new and interesting people. Indeed, it was just as the Canadian couple that we met over breakfast in Wylam had predicted I would feel after several days on the trail.

The cost of a one-way train ticket from Carlisle to London was about $200, which seemed very expensive. Dave shrugged his shoulders and explained that no one really understood the pricing of passenger rail in the aftermath of the British Rail privatization that had been rolled out in the mid to late 1990s.

As the night fell open us and we rumbled through the Lake District and hurtled south towards London, we basked quietly in our accomplishment. The mileage covered in five and a half days was not to be sniffed at, particularly given our age and the constant rainfall. I wished we had squeezed in an additional day or two to give us time to soak in the treasures of Birdoswald and Vindolanda, but we were both at the mercy of our tight work schedules.

The train slowly filled up as we made our stops along the West Coast Main Line—Preston, Crewe, Nuneaton ... large, ornately dressed Hindu families; young couples with cans of lager "pre-gaming" before hitting the London nightclubs; disheveled tourists trying to read or nod off.

The range and quality of alcoholic refreshments on the inter-city train service has improved immeasurably over the decades since the 1970s when the only "booze" available would typically be bitter, brown ale or lager. In the present day inter city trains in the UK still do not, and possibly never will, run with the metronomic punctuality of Swiss InterCity railways or the comfort and efficiency of Deutsche Bahn's IC service, but at least we can offer the world a pleasing array of refreshments whilst we eventually get you to your ultimate destination. "Keep quaffing and carry on," one might say with due apologies to our famous wartime rallying cry of "keep calm and carry on."

I decided to walk down to the dining cab at the end of the train to get a celebratory glass or two of wine. Just before the bar area, I noticed a commotion and looked down to see a small boy, maybe four years old. He was on top of his sister, who was maybe half his age, having the best of it in a sibling-wrestling match whilst multi-tasking by also furiously playing with his toy car. As I approached, balancing our supplies of wine and gin, I looked across at a young lady who I soon learned to be his mother. I recognized and immediately empathized with her exhausted and resigned expression—she was hostage to the reality that her hyperactive offspring would continue to slug it out until they dropped. She was probably grateful to have the opportunity to sink into a seat on the train for a couple of hours and a chance to let the kids heatedly and anarchically make their own fun. I decided that I would attempt to intricately tiptoe around the spaghetti-junction of flailing arms and legs rather than requesting them to move. At the time laden down with our alcoholic sustenance, it felt as challenging to edge around them without contact as it did to negotiate any of the narrow or steep nooks and crannies I encountered along the Path. In the course of maneuvering past them, the boy looked up from his pugilistic play-date and shot me an enraged glare and spewed out in a broad "Brummie" (Birmingham) accent, "oi, what are you doing, you fat wanker?" He then returned to his dual pursuits of playing with his toy and continuing his seemingly endless internecine version of WWE SmackDown. The young lady, his mom, half-heartedly reprimanded her boy with a "Wayne, don't be so rude," before returning to her shattered thousand-meter stare. As I continued to my seat, with wine and gin supplies mercifully intact, I really couldn't do anything but smile to myself and think back to how my own son, Calum, who the boy reminded me of at a similar age, would enthusiastically and manically conduct fights between his toy Batman and stegosaurus models whilst also thinking nothing of playing rough and tumble with considerably bigger boys at school. Calum, in comparison, was always a model of politeness, but I decided that the boy on the train was in several ways like he often was—just having noisy fun, possibly over-tired and not really doing anyone any harm—just boisterously enjoying his childhood. And as for his mom, well she was just pursuing a version of that same "conscientiously aloof" approach to child minding which I had employed when looking after Mark's, a friend's and my own kids whilst they watched Jumanji *all those years before in Georgia—so who am I to judge?*

I later told Dave that this incident reminded me of the story behind one of David Bowie's music videos that he recounted years later. The crew was filming the video on the streets of London, and Bowie was dressed in one of his bizarre and operatic Venetian clown outfits. An old man happened across the scene and actually caused an interruption in the filming. Bowie sat on a bench as one of the production crew pointed to him and asked the old man if he knew who he (Bowie) was. "Some old c**t dressed like a clown," was his response.

This represented England at its best to me. As soon as one starts to swell with self-regard, there is always someone else eager to pierce all misplaced pride and vanity and provide the needed reminder that all of our accomplishments are built on sand.

As London approached, and Mark and I continued to shoot the breeze and trade war stories over our Virgin Trains "in-flight" drinks, I had the chance to reflect upon our shared experience and that rather than just ruminating about it, we made it happen. I thought back to one of my original questions of what "kind of England" I would find during our week as itinerant hikers. Of course this is too big a question to ever be satisfied with a single answer. Nonetheless the people we had met had generally been kind and generous with their time and reinforced my view that the supposed north-south divide in England was an exaggeration on a human level at least. Passing-by the vicinity of the "Remain" constituencies of South Lakeland, Manchester, Stockport, Warwick and Stevenage, I even found myself doing the opposite of my despondent listing of Leave-voting towns on our northbound journey the previous Saturday and attempting a more philosophical take on Brexit. For certain now the door was shut and the European horse had bolted. The most important thing is my love of Europe, its constituent parts, and my belief that how we interact on a human level is what makes a society strong and worth having rather than its political infrastructure. In a small way, the kind people who we had met during the week in the quiet villages of Northumberland and Cumbria, away from the London metropolis, had positively reinforced this notion.

By the time we got back to my home in Kew, Ben's Good Wine Shop had closed for the evening, so were unable to stage our Phileas Fogg–style homecoming at our East India Club equivalent. So we settled for phoning through an order to a nearby Indian restaurant, to be washed down with several of my wife's killer gin concoctions. And after that it would be back to regular London life spiced up by following England's latest quest to land the Rugby World Cup in Japan. My plans to travel out to see them play in Yokohama were thwarted by Typhoon Hagibis but my disappointment was nothing in comparison to the devastation suffered by many Japanese families as a result of the storm. As for England, they were great in the quarters and semis, but were mercilessly overpowered by our old friends from South Africa in the final proving once again that it can be better to travel than to arrive!

Postscript

"Around CE 165, the Anatolian town of Hierapolis erected a statue to the god Apollo Alexikakos, the Averter of Evil, so that the people might be spared from a terrible new infectious disease with utterly gruesome symptoms. Victims were known to endure fever, chills, upset stomach and diarrhea that turned from red to black over the course of a week. They also developed horrible black pocks over their bodies, both inside and out, that scabbed over and left disfiguring scars."[1]

The pandemic that struck what is now modern-day Turkey 45 year after the completion of Hadrian's Wall was most likely an attack of smallpox. Before it had finished burning its way through the Roman Empire, it left an estimated 10 percent of the population dead, and the bewildered survivors undoubtedly physically weakened and traumatized. At its peak, it killed an estimated 2,000 people a day in the city of Rome alone.

While Rome suffered tremendously from its losses, it was blessed with the good fortune of having an extraordinarily competent emperor, Marcus Aurelius, who was, like Hadrian, a follower of Stoicism. He ruled according to that philosophy's tenets, which stressed self-restraint, reason, and a deep and abiding respect for nature. He was considered the last of the "Five Good Emperors," who, despite their absolute power, served Rome well by stressing peace and prosperity for almost one hundred years.

Despite the unprecedented horror created by the pestilence, Rome quickly adapted to the new realities; Emperor Marcus Aurelius, great nephew to Hadrian, invited immigrants outside the empire to replace both workers lost in the cities and the farmers whose fields would have otherwise been left fallow. Slaves and gladiators were recruited to replace the legionnaires cut down by the disease. In short, Rome proved resilient to an existential threat that, absent adept and flexible leadership, might easily have led to its collapse. But instead, it rose to the challenge and continued to flourish for much of its remaining 300 years. After the fall of the Republic, Rome was generally blessed with capable leadership from its emperors (with the notable exceptions of Nero and Caligula) until the death of Marcus Aurelius. Inevitably, this lucky streak finally came to an end.

The uneven and fitful response to the Corona virus was largely driven by politics and was symptomatic of a broken society that could not even unite in the face of a deadly public health crisis. Mistrust of competence, science, and expertise have helped inflame a destructive hyper individualism that masquerades as "freedom." As many have pointed out, it is safe to assume that if World War II broke out now with today's prevailing attitudes, a goodly portion of our population would never adhere to such common-sense measures as blackouts and rationing.

Dave and I both went into lockdown (or "house arrest," as Dave described it) in the middle of March of 2020 due to the Covid-19 virus; we were fortunate—our jobs allowed us to work from home, which was actually a welcomed development to a committed introvert like me.

In contrast to this, the UK education system was thrown into disarray. My son's university degree was to be decided by a mathematical formula, cobbled together in haste by the university authorities and which was intended to accurately reflect four years of academic endeavor. It fell some way short of its goal, but at least he emerged from the experience as a trilingual graduate lead guitarist still smashing out "face-melting" solos and recorded a new album. The high school exams which my daughter was due to take were cancelled, after which the fun really began when the original attempt at

---

an algorithm-based replacement grading system met with universal public outcry and had to be reversed. My daughter even appeared on the front page of The Times *newspaper carrying a banner and looking judgmentally furious at a protest in Parliament Square, Westminster against the new grading construct.*

Although my professional life was as busy as ever following the Covid-19 outbreak it did prompt me to think back to our time at Hadrian's Wall, and how the freedom which afforded us the opportunity to have our week there and indeed to write this book is something we take for granted. It was quite reassuring to observe my parents' reaction to lockdown. Both now in their 90s, their response was pure World War II in nature with a pragmatic "Keep calm and carry on" mantra to the fore. They kept their spirits up despite the fact that Zoom calls and other forms of video link which almost overnight have come into common use for many of us, are not an option for them and it would be a long time before we would be able to see each other again.

Small businesses around the UK were severely affected by lockdown—Ben, the irrepressible Geordie owner of the fabulous wine and cheese shop in Kew Gardens in London, was forced to shutter, although I was pleased to hear that he was, according to Dave, "still punching," establishing a home delivery service during the most harrowing period of the disease's spread in the spring. He ultimately reopened following the relaxation of lockdown in the summer to welcome back his relieved local fan base and even opened an additional shop in nearby Richmond, which was voted Decanter's Best London Neighbourhood Wine Shop. Our "East India Club" moves on to a new chapter.

Hadrian's Wall provides a strong economic boost to the sparsely populated towns and villages that are dotted along its Path. The bed and breakfasts, pubs, and museums have suffered greatly since Britain went into lockdown, and the Hadrian's Wall Heritage website provided information on assistance that could be provided to struggling local businesses.

I watched with interest as the British election returns were presented on the BBC in December 2019. Ian Levy, the newly elected Conservative Party Cumbrian MP for Blyth Valley (the first from his party to win in that constituency in generations), thundered in his victory speech: "we weel git BRAKE-sit doon." And at the time of writing the UK continues its troubled progression towards Brexit albeit with the form of final departure from the EU still in the melting pot, and with its timing conceivably prolonged by the pressures of the Covid crisis. I was heartened to see the humor that the pro–EU Scots infused into the situation, with some waggishly suggesting that Hadrian's Wall should be rebuilt, and England "would pay for it." For entertainment during my downtime, I watched the prescient 2008 post-apocalyptic film *Doomsday* where England rebuilt the Wall to quarantine Scots suffering from a deadly virus.

I admired the poised and dignified performance of Fiona Hill—a North Country native and expert on Russian affairs—during the Trump impeachment hearings. She handled the grillings she received from hostile congressmen with customary northern English directness and aplomb.

Spring quickly merged into summer as the months became a blur and the pandemic ebbed and flowed with predictable flare-ups occurring in areas that pre-maturely relaxed restrictions based on politics, an honest desire to jump start economic growth, or simply sheer exhaustion from lockdown fatigue. One sports season after another was either cancelled or truncated with games played in stadiums and arenas in front of few or no fans. Small businesses that I had loved and frequented for decades hung on grimly for as long as they could, but all too many ultimately shut their doors forever.

The autumn brought little in the way of relief. The West Coast burned with apocalyptic fury, as the smoke and haze from forest fires could be seen as far away as London. The hurricane season extended into late October and even early November, as the Gulf Coast was lashed with one severe storm after another. Global warming, like the pandemic, did not care if one believed it was "fake" or not. Warmer waters exhausted the twenty-six women and men's names used for the hurricane and tropical storm season, and we were forced to switch to the Greek alphabet to tag subsequent storms. Hurricane Zeta struck the Louisiana coast and raced inland, knocking out power in our Atlanta neighborhood, 250 miles distant from any ocean shoreline, for three days.

The November 3 election left both sides strangely unhappy. Those who voted against Trump were hoping for a full-fledged renunciation of inward-looking right-wing nativism and populism, and those on the right believed until the end (and even well after the end) that their man would prevail. Neither side achieved their most ambitious goals, so we head into 2021 with divided government that promises more anger, recrimination, and agonizing stalemate.

For the first time, I began to seriously think that our Republic might no longer survive the internal pressure of two sides that, if they are honest, despise each other with more intensity than any potential foreign enemy. The sense of a common bond forged by years of shared history is in danger of being shattered by two sets of values that are diametrically opposed to each other and absolutely unyielding. I was, like Dave and Brexit, exhausted by the struggle that shows no sign of ending, and that I fear will inevitably lead to bloodshed. In my more defeated and fanciful moments, I daydream of emigration with a fresh start, spending my remaining years trying to restore a Sicilian cottage or owning a hostelry near the Wall Path, welcoming wet and exhausted hikers in to take shelter from the never-ending downpours. In my more optimistic moments, I remain determined to stay and fight for the survival of the Republic against those who view democracy as dispensable in their search for power.

In his 2020 campaign, President Trump continued to call for expansion of the wall covering the almost 2,000-mile Mexican border. It remained to be seen if his vision of a bristling barrier covering hundreds of miles over river and desert would ever come to fruition.

The early returns of the newly finished portions were not encouraging—enterprising migrants were using cheap saws to cut their way through the "beautiful" wall.

All walls ultimately fail, even one as sturdily built and heavily manned as Hadrian's Wall. Early in the 5th century CE, the Romans left Britain for good, crossing the English Channel into Gaul in an unsuccessful attempt to beat back Germanic invaders threatening the Empire's heartland. There is evidence that both the Romano-British natives and the invading Anglo-Saxons attempted to restore some military utility to the Wall, but by the 6th century CE it had started its slow decline into obsolescence and decay

The Romans left Britain with the Wall and many other relics that we still admire for their artistry, innovation and durability. More importantly Rome bequeathed to Britain an enduring legacy of competent government, law and order, industry, and education. There was some regression after the Romans left—glass making, for instance, did not re-emerge until the 13th century, and the use of the Latin language was confined to a small minority of educated priests and nobility.

I remember reading once that if we know when a physical object was created, we can accurately predict its end date with some degree of accuracy; anything observable has a 50 percent probability of having completed 25–75 percent of its life span. The statistician who developed this simple formula used it to predict the date for the fall of the Berlin Wall with remarkable accuracy. I think back to my experience with the Berlin Wall, in 1980, and how nothing in the world would have convinced me at that time that that bristling and horrendously ugly barrier had less of a decade before it, too, would be smashed to the ground. All walls, like all things and all people, are ephemeral and have pre-loaded expiration dates.

More than anything, walls may provide the builders and those who feel protected by them with a sense of psychological security merely by their stunning architecture—the guarded barriers stretching through cityscapes, mountains, deserts and riverbanks demonstrate consistency and linearity in a world that seems otherwise unmoored and random.

They also offer the promise of a better life to those being contained or kept out. Mongolian tribes studying and simply maneuevering around the Great Wall in the north of China during the time of Genghis Khan, East Berliners waking up to a hastily built and crudely constructed concrete partition in 1961 and Palestinians staring at the high tech West Bank Barrier today all must have wondered why so much effort was expended for the walls' construction, and what sort of improvements in their lives await them on the other side.

The only certainty is that some time in the future, if the planet survives in the centuries ahead, the ruins of the Mexican border wall will attract the curious and the solemn, who will stroll with wonder amongst its Ozymandian remains. They will scan the records and posit opinions on what prompted a people to build such a barrier.

In my more optimistic moments, I believe that the human psyche will have shifted so much by then that they will be completely dumbfounded that their distant ancestors ever seriously considered such a project. But I doubt it. As the German philosopher Friedrich Hegel once said, "The only thing we learn from history is that we learn nothing from history."

Chapter Notes

Chapter 1

1. "Not Quite a Geordie," The Folk Ethnonyms of North-East England, Michael Pearce, University of Sunderland, December 2014, https://www.researchgate.net/publication/338254202_%27Not_quite_a_Geordie%27_the_folk-ethnonyms_of_north-east_England_Nomina_37_ISSN_0141_6340, accessed 10/22/2020.

2. "Geordie Guide—Defining Geordie," Newcastle University Library, www.libguides.ncl.ac.uk, accessed October 28, 2020.

3. Henry Stedman and Daniel McCrohan, Hadrian's Wall Path (Hindhead, Surrey: Trailblazer Publishers, 5th Edition, 2017), pages 7–8.

4. "Hadrian's Wall Path," Te Araroa, New Zealand's Trail Website, https://www.teararoa.org.nz/hadrianswallpath/, accessed October 22, 2019.

5. "Bharati Buys Out British Shipyard Major Swan Hunter," Business Standard, April 10, 2007, https://www.business-standard.com/company/bharati-defence-23505/information/company-history; accessed October 23, 2019.

6. Richard Caendish, "Launch of the Mauretania," History Today, Volume 56, Issue 9, September 2006, https://www.historytoday.com/archive/launch-mauretania, accessed July 4, 2020.

7. Allan's Tyneside Songs, 1891, https://openlibrary.org/books/OL23493459M/Allan%27s_Illustrated_Edition_of_Tyneside_Songs_and_Readings_With_Lives_Portraits, accessed September 19, 2020.

8. Museums Northumberland, www.museumsnorthumberland.org.uk/woodhorn-museum, accessed on September 17, 2020.

9. William Feaver, "Anyone Can Paint," The Guardian, January 24, 2009, https://www.theguardian.com/artanddesign/2009/jan/24/pitmen-painters-national-theatre, accessed September 17, 2020.

10. Anthony Burton, "TV Walks—Hadrian's Wall Path National Trail," August 1, 2007, www.tvwalks.com, accessed July 4, 2020.

11. North East War Memorials Project, 2020, www. http://www.newmp.org.uk/, accessed October 28, 2020.

12. Northumberland Communities, https://communities.northumberland.gov.uk/Wylam_Census.htm, accessed October 28, 2020.

13. Ibid.

14. Review of the novel Learning to Fly by V.M. Taylor, The Northumbrian, August 9, 2017: 7, https://www.thenorthumbrian.co.uk/2017/08/09/page/2/, accessed November 15, 2020.

15. Paul Kingsnorth, Real England: The Battle Against the Bland (London: Portobello Books, First Edition, 2009), page 152.

16. Rob Davies and Richard Partington, "More Than 25% of UK Pubs Have Closed Since 2001," The Guardian, November 26, 2018, https://www.theguardian.com/business/2018/nov/26/uk-pub-closures-financial-crisis-birmingham-ons-figures, accessed October 29, 2019.

17. Paul Kingsnorth, Real England: The

Battle Against the Bland (London: Portobello Books, First Edition, 2009), page 26.

18. "Who Owns What in the UK Brewing Scene?" Thought Piece—The Carling Team, https://www.carlingpartnership.com/insights/who-owns-what-in-the-uk-brewing-scene/, accessed October 30, 2019.

19. Richard Partington, "Brexit Will Hit North of England the Hardest, Says Thinktank," *The Guardian*, November 9, 2017, https://amp.theguardian.com/business/2017/nov/09/brexit-will-hit-northern-england-economy-hardest-ippr-north-thinktank, accessed November 7, 2019

20. "Hagg Bank Bridge," Northumbria.Info, http://www.northumbria.info/Pages/haggbnkbr.html, accessed October 28, 2020.

Chapter 2

1. Claire Bates, "When Foot and Mouth Disease Stopped Britain in Its Tracks," *BBC News Magazine*, February 16, 2016, https://www.bbc.com/news/magazine-35581830, accessed November 22, 2019.

2. Pipe Rolls, National Archives, www.nationalarchives.co.uk, accessed September 13, 2020.

3. Heddon-on-the-Wall Local History Society, www.heddonhistory.weebly.com, accessed October 28, 2020.

4. John Wesley, *The Journal of John Wesley* (Chicago: Moody Press, 1951), page 115.

5. History of Heddon-on-the-Wall, English Heritage, https://www.english-heritage.org.uk/visit/places/heddon-on-the-wall-hadrians-wall/history/, accessed November 2, 2019.

6. Adrian Goldsworthy, *Hadrian's Wall* (New York: Basic Books, First Edition, 2018), page 25.

7. Edward Gibbon, *Decline and Fall of the Roman Empire* (Bury, 1909), page 78.

8. Marguerite Yourcenar, *Memoirs of Hadrian* (New York: Farrar, Straus, and Giroux, paperback edition, 2005), page 95.

9. Kenneth O. Morgan, ed., *The Oxford Illustrated History of Britain* (Oxford: Oxford University Press, reprint, 1994), page 22.

10. H.H. Ben-Sasson, *A History of the Jewish People* (Cambridge: Harvard University Press, 1976), page 334.

11. Adrian Goldsworthy, *Hadrian's Wall* (New York: Basic Books 2018), page 20.

12. Adrian Goldsworthy, *Caesar: Life of a Colossus* (New Haven: Yale University Press, 2006), page 285.

13. Squirrels in the UK, The Wildlife Trust, https://www.wildlifetrusts.org/saving-species/red-squirrels, accessed August 29, 2020.

14. Patrick Barkhaam, "Red squirrels: 5,000 volunteers sought to save species—and help kill invasive greys," *The Guardian*, February 24, 2017, https://www.theguardian.com/environment/2017/feb/24/red-squirrels-5000-volunteers-sought-to-save-species-and-help-kill-invasive-greys, accessed August 29, 2020.

15. Paul Kingsnorth, *Real England: The Battle Against the Bland* (London: Portobello Books, First Edition, 2009), page 152.

16. Tim Radford, "Warning Sounded on Decline of Species," *The Guardian*, March 19, 2004.

17. Paul Kingsnorth, *Real England: The Battle Against the Bland* (London: Portobello Books, First Edition, 2009), page 152.

18. "Cow Injures Man on Hadrian's Wall Trek," https://www.irwinmitchell.com/client-stories/2012/may/cow-injures-man-on-hadrian-s-wall-trek, accessed August 19, 2020.

19. Tom Rowley, "Walking the Wall: My Brexit Hike in Northern England," *The Economist*, https://www.economist.com/1843/2019/12/04/walking-the-wall-my-brexit-hike-in-northern-england, accessed September 5, 2020.

20. Heavenfield-St. Oswald's Church, Britain Express, https://www.britainexpress.com/counties/northumbria/churches/heavenfield.htm, accessed November 5, 2019.

21. Michelle Goldberg, "The Darkness Where the World Should Be," *The New York Times*, January 24, 2020, https://www.nytimes.com/2020/01/24/opinion/sunday/william-gibson-agency.html, accessed August 29, 2020.

22. George Orwell, *The Road to Wigan Pier* (New York: A Harvest Book—Harcourt, Jovanovich, 1958), page 192.

Chapter 3

1. Adrian Goldsworthy, *Hadrian's Wall* (New York: Basic Books, First Edition, 2018), page xiii.

2. *Ibid.*, pages 293–95.

3. Hunter Davies, *A Walk Along the Wall: A Journey Along Hadrian's Wall* (London: Orion Books, paperback edition, 2000), page 108.

4. Paul Elliott, *Everyday Life of a Soldier on Hadrian's Wall* (Oxford: Fonthill Media Limited, 2019), page 15.

5. *Ibid.*, page 99.

6. "The Geography of Strabo," *Loeb Classical Library Edition*, Vol. II, 1923, Book IV, Chapter V. http://penelope.uchicago.edu/Thayer/e/roman/texts/strabo/4e*.html, accessed October 18, 2020.

7. Nic Fields, *Hadrian's Wall AD 122 –410* (Oxford: Osprey Publishing, 2003), pages 49–52.

8. Nigel Cross, "Food in Romano Britain," Resourcesforhistory.com, https://resourcesforhistory.com/Roman_Food_in_Britain.htm, accessed August 8, 2020.

9. W.E. Lunt, *History of England* (New York: Harper and Brothers, Fourth Edition, 1957), page 28.

10. Daniel Defoe, *A True Collection of the Writings of the Author of The True Born English-man: Corrected by Himself* (London, 1703), pages 101–01.

11. Cassius Dio, Roman History, Epitome of Book LXXVII, Vol. IX, page 239, https://penelope.uchicago.edu/Thayer/E/Roman/Texts/Cassius_Dio/77*.html, accessed August 30, 2020.

12. Paul Elliott, *Everyday Life of a Soldier on Hadrian's Wall* (Oxford: Fonthill Media Limited, 2019), page 147.

13. Hunter Davies, *A Walk Along the Wall: A Journey Along Hadrian's Wall* (London: Orion Books, paperback edition, 2000), pages 1071–08.

14. Dr. Simon Elliott, "The Campaigns of Septimius Severus in the Far North of Britain," https://www.youtube.com/watch?v=TV4oXWk3jxs&t=3601s, accessed August 29, 2020.

15. *Ibid.*

16. "Game of Thrones Bid to Boost Hadrian's Wall Visits," BBC News, March 19, 2019, https://www.bbc.com/news/uk-england-47624086, accessed July 9, 2020.

17. Henry Stedman and Daniel McCrohan, *Hadrian's Wall Path* (Hindhead, Surrey: Trailblazer Publishers, 5th Edition, 2017), page 153.

18. Rudyard Kipling, "A Song to Mithras Hymn of the XXX Legion: circa A.D. 350 On the Great Wall," *Puck of Pook's Hill* (1906), https://telelib.com/authors/K/KiplingRudyard/verse/p2/mithras.html, accessed September 1, 2020.

19. Adrian Goldsworthy, *Hadrian's Wall* (New York: Basic Books, First Edition, 2018), page 39.

20. Owen Bowcott, Ben Quinn and Severin Carrell, "Johnson's suspension of Parliament unlawful, supreme court rules," *The Guardian*, September 24, 2019, accessed November 22, 2020.

21. Adam Taylor, "Boris Johnson or Donald Trump: Whose Day Was Worse," *The Spokesman Review*, September 24, 2019, last updated October 31, 2019, accessed November 1, 2020.

22. Donald L. Wasson, "Roman Citizenship," *Ancient History Encyclopedia*, January 27, 2016, https://www.ancient.eu/article/859/roman-citizenship/, accessed November 16, 2019.

23. Adrian Goldsworthy, *Caesar: Life of a Colossus* (New Haven: Yale University Press, 2006), page 23.

24. Edward J. Watts, *Mortal Republic: How Rome Fell Into Tyranny* (New York: Basic Books, 2018), page 58.

25. National Trail—Hadrian's Wall Path, Harvey Maps Company.

26. David Hackett Fischer, *Albion's*

Seed: Four British Folkways in America (New York: Oxford University Press, 1989), page 626.

27. *Ibid.*, page 6.

28. *Ibid.*, page 622.

29. *Ibid.*, page 650.

30. *Ibid.*, page 614.

31. *Ibid.*, page 834.

32. *Ibid.*, page 662.

33. *Ibid.*, page 654.

34. Henry Stedman and Daniel McCrohan, *Hadrian's Wall Path* (Hindhead, Surrey: Trailblazer Publishers, 5th Edition, 2017), page 158.

35. W.H. Auden, *Collected Poems*, edited by Edward Mendelson (New York: Vintage International, 1991), page 143.

36. Milecastle 38, Hadrian's Wall and the "Dutch Bankers," https://www.nationaltrail.co.uk/sites/default/files/best_of_both_worlds_case_study_dutch_bankers_pdf.pdf, accessed January 29, 2020.

37. Erin Blackmore, "Who's Digging Up Hadrian's Wall?" *Smithsonian Magazine*, February 12, 2015, https://www.smithsonianmag.com/smart-news/whos-digging-hadrians-wall-180954235/, accessed August 19, 2020.

38. Dalya Alberge, "Hadrian's Wall Dig Reveals Oldest Christian Graffiti on Chalice," *The Guardian*, August 29, 2020.

39. Rupert Millar, "Send Beer! The Romans in North Britain," *The Drinks Business*, July 12, 2017.

40. Jason Daley, "Archaeologists Uncover an Ancient Roman gamed board at Hadrian's Wall," Smithsonian Magazine, smithsonianmag.com, May 8, 2019, accessed November 15, 2020.

41. Henry Stedman and Daniel McCrohan, *Hadrian's Wall Path* (Hindhead, Surrey: Trailblazer Publishers, 5th Edition, 2017), page 160.

Chapter 4

1. "Recalling UK's Warmest and Wettest December," *The Guardian*, December 16, 2019, https://www.theguardian.com/news/2019/dec/16/recalling-uks-warm est-and-wettest-december, accessed March 5, 2020.

2. Hunter Davies, *A Walk Along the Wall: A Journey Along Hadrian's Wall* (London: Orion Books, paperback edition, 2000), page 173.

3. *Ibid.*, page 172.

4. *Ibid.*, page 173.

5. Lewis Spence, *The Magic Arts in Celtic Britain* (Mineola, New York: Dover Publications, 1999), page 147.

6. "Hadrian's Wall Completed by Man in Trunks and Roman Helmet," bbc.co.uk, accessed October 28, 2020, https://www.bbc.co.uk/news/uk-england-glou cestershire.

7. Rob Davies, "British Pub Numbers Grow for the First Time in a Decade," *The Guardian*, December 10, 2019.

8. John Major speech to the Conservative Group for Europe, April 22, 1993, Oxford Reference, https://www.oxfordreference.com/view/10.1093/acref/9780191826719.001.0001/q-oro-ed40-0007018, accessed July 5, 2020.

9. Jeremy Paxman, *The English: A Portrait of a People* (London: Penguin Books, 1999), page 149.

10. Eric S. Wood, *Historical Britain* (London: The Harvill Press, 1995), page 41.

11. Elli Thomas, Ilona Serwicka and Paul Swinney, Centre for Cities, Urban, July 2015, https://www.centreforcities.org/wp-content/uploads/2015/07/150-72-0-Urban-Demographics.pdf, accessed September 1, 2020.

12. William Blake,"Milton Poem, copy B object 2," The William Blake Archive, ed. Morris Eaves, Robert N. Essick, and Joseph Viscomi, http://www.blakearchive.org/copy/milton.b?descId=milton.b.il lbk.02 accessed September 2, 2020.

13. "Walton on the Roman Wall," from "Musings in the Dark: Poems and Songs," by James Steele, published in 1871.

Chapter 5

1. Henry Stedman and Daniel McCrohan, *Hadrian's Wall Path* (Hindhead,

Surrey: Trailblazer Publishers, 5th Edition, 2017), pages 189–190.

2. Cumbria Intelligence Observatory quoting Office for National Statistics, 2019, https://www.cumbriaobservatory.org.uk/population/report/view, accessed October 29, 2020.

3. BBC, "Carlisle Gets Its Own Version of the Game Monopoly," http://www.bbc.co.uk/cumbria/content/articles/2007/10/24/carlisle_monopoly_video_feature.shtml#:~:text=Carlisle%20Castle%20saw%20the%20launch,at%20the%20%C2%A3400%20spot, last modified September 24, 2014, accessed October 29, 2020.

4. Kenneth Jackson, *Language and History in Early Britain* (Edinburgh: Edinburgh University Press, 1953), page 39.

5. Encyclopaedia Britannica, Ninth Edition, "Carlisle (1.)," https://en.wikisource.org/wiki/Encyclopædia_Britannica,_Ninth_Edition/Carlisle_(1.), accessed October 23, 2020.

6. Phil Mellows, "The Carlisle Experiment—The Extraordinary Story of Nationalized Pubs During the First World War," *The Morning Advertiser*, July 25, 2016, https://www.morningadvertiser.co.uk/Article/2016/07/25/The-extraordinary-story-of-nationalised-pubs-during-the-First-World-War, accessed October 14, 2020.

Chapter 6

1. *The Living Wall*, 1974, Tyne Tees Television, http://www.yorkshirefilmarchive.com/film/living-wall, accessed September 6, 2020.

2. William Hutton, *The History of the Roman Wall Which Crosses the Island of Britain from the German Ocean to the Irish Sea* (London: John Nichols & Son, 1802), page 1.

3. "MOD 'Places' Its Toxic Tank Shells in Solway Firth," *The Herald*, March 9, 2013, https://www.heraldscotland.com/news/13095462.mod-places-its-toxic-tank-shells-in-solway-firth/, accessed April 28, 2020.

4. Giancarlo Rinaldi, "Solway Junction Railway; The Ill-fated Scotland to England Rail Route," https://www.bbc.co.uk/news/uk-scotland-south-scotland, September 13, 2019, accessed October 29, 2020.

5. Amy Brough, "Legend of the Blacksmiths Anvil Priest," https://www.gretnagreen.com/legend-of-the-blacksmiths-anvil-priest, Gretna Green, August 11, 2015, accessed October 29, 2020.

6. *Billy Connolly's World Tour of England Wales and Ireland*, BBC TV, 2002.

7. Kevin Bridges, *Live at the Referendum*, BBC TV, September 2014.

8. Samuel Johnson, *Dictionary of the English Language*, Volume II (London: T.T. and J. Tegg, 1833), page 215.

9. William Hutton, *The History of the Roman Wall Which Crosses the Island of Britain from the German Ocean to the Irish Sea* (London: John Nichols & Son, 1802), The Eighteenth Station.

10. Kirsten Henton, "The Tiny Country Between England and Scotland," BBC Travel, May 5, 2020, http://www.bbc.com/travel/story/20200504-the-tiny-country-between-england-and-scotland?ocid=fbtvl, accessed June 11, 2020.

11. Henry Stedman and Daniel McCrohan, *Hadrian's Wall Path* (Hindhead, Surrey: Trailblazer Publishers, 5th Edition, 2017), page 208.

Postscript

1. Edward Watts, Zócalo Public Square, Smithsonianmag.com, April 28, 2020, accessed May 10, 2020, https://www.smithsonianmag.com/history/what-rome-learned-deadly-antonine-plague-165-d-180974758/?utm_source=smithsonian daily&utm_medium=email&utm_campaign=20200428-daily-.

Bibliography

Auden, W.H. *Collected Poems.* Mendelson, Edward, ed. New York: Vintage International, 1991.

Cross, Nigel. "Food in Romano Britain." Resourcesforhistory.com, https://resources forhistory.com/Roman_Food_in_Britain.htm, 2006.

Davies, Hunter. *A Walk Along the Wall: A Journey Along Hadrian's Wall.* London: Orion Books, paperback edition, 2000.

Elliott, Paul. *Everyday Life of a Soldier on Hadrian's Wall.* Oxford: Fonthill Media Limited, 2019.

Fields, Nic. *Hadrian's Wall AD 122–400.* Oxford: Osprey Publishing, 2003.

Fischer, David Hackett. *Albion's Seed: Four British Folkways in America.* New York: Oxford University Press, 1989.

Goldsworthy, Adrian. *Caesar: Life of a Colossus.* New Haven: Yale University Press, 2006.

_____. *Hadrian's Wall.* New York: Basic Books, 2018.

Hutton, William. *The History of the Roman Wall Which Crosses the Island of Britain from the German Ocean to the Irish Sea.* London: John Nichols & Son, 1802, The Eighteenth Station.

Kingsnorth, Paul. *Real England: The Battle Against the Bland.* London: Portobello Books, Ltd., 2009.

Morgan, Kenneth O. *The Oxford Illustrated History of Britain.* Oxford: Oxford University Press, reprint, 1994.

Paxman, Jeremy. *The English: A Portrait of a People.* London: Penguin Books, 1999.

Stedman, Henry, and Daniel McCrohan. *Hadrian's Wall Path.* Hindhead, Surrey: United Trailblazer Publishers, 5th Edition, 2017.

Watts, Edward J. *Mortal Republic: How Rome Fell into Tyranny.* New York: Basic Books, 2018.

Wood, Eric S. *Historical Britain.* London: The Harvill Press, 1995.

Index

Albion (Romano) 86
Almond, David (writer) 33
Amis, Martin (writer) 124
AMRO Bank ("Dutch bankers" affair) 112–113
"Angel of the North" (monument) 33–34
Anglo-Saxons 76, 184
Antinous (Emperor Hadrian's lover) 65
Antonine Wall 67
Antoninus Pius (Roman emperor) 67
Appalachia, Appalachians 108–110
Appalachian Trail ("AT") 1, 27, 35, 48, 80, 96, 110, 115, 153, 159, 161
Armstrong, Neil (United States astronaut) 109
Arthur ("Once and Future King of England") 140–141, 168
Ashington Group (group of Northumbrian artists) 41
Athens, Georgia music scene (B-52's, Love Tractor, Pylon, REM) 125
Atlanta, Georgia: 138, 174, 183; travels to 125, 128–129
Atlee, Clement (United Kingdom prime minister) 53
Auden, W.H. (poet) 112; *The Roman Wall Blues* 112; *Twelve Songs* 112
Augustus Caesar (Roman emperor) 106
Austin Powers (film series) 4
Australia: Sydney 25

Bannockburn, Battle of 20
Bar Kokhba Revolt (destruction of Jewish Temple) 67
baseball (sport) 126, 128, 130, 132
Bath (city in Somerset; "Aquae Sulis") 8
Beaumont (town in Cumbria) 172
"Ben" (Kew's Good Wine Shop) 15–16, 178, 181
Berlin, Germany: travels to 26; Wall 26, 65, 185–186
Biden, Joseph (United States president) 102

Blake, William (poet) 146–147
Bonnie Prince Charlie (Charles Edward Stuart) 72, 119, 157, 164
border country 1, 106–109
Bowie, David 20, 130, 177
Bowness-on-Solway (town in Cumbria) 17, 77, 140, 142, 160–161, 163, 165–168
Branagh, Kenneth (actor) 81
Braveheart (film) 171
"Brexit" 50, 54–57, 102, 123, 145, 166, 178, 182–183
Brighton and Hove Albion F.C. "Seagulls" 23
Brighton Pavilion 17
Britannia (Roman province) 7, 66–68, 86–87
Burgh-by-Sands (town in Cumbria) 171; St. Michael's Church 171
Bush, George H.W. (United States president) 81
Busy Gap Rogues 106; *see also* Hadrian's Wall

Calais, France 3
Caledonia and Caledonians 6, 67–68, 86, 89, 91–92, 110–111; *see also* Celts; Picts; Scots
Caligula (Roman emperor) 180
Cameron, David (former United Kingdom Prime Minister) 54
Canadian (bank) 15, 80, 126
Capp, Andy (Reg Smythe character) 30
Carlisle (city in Cumbria) 35, 61, 68, 78, 141, 153, 155, 157; Bonnie Prince Charlie invasion of 72, 164; Botchergate 158; Brazuca 1 Grooming Shop (barber shop) 160; Debenham's 174; Roman Wall 5, 16; Spider and Fly (restaurant) 160; train station 174
Cassius Dio (Roman historian) 89
Celts (people) 6, 90
Centurion (film) 68
Charles I (King of England) 106

Cheviot Hills (uplands in the border country) 95
Christie, Agatha (writer) 146
Churchill, Winston (United Kingdom prime minister) 53, 122
Clayton, John 110; Clayton Wall 111
Cleese, John (comedian): as Basil Fawlty in *Fawlty Towers* 163; as Reg in *Life of Brian* 11
Clegg, Tess (daughter of co-author) 131–132
coal mining, collieries 24, 40–41, 43
Cologne, Germany 5
Common, Jack (novelist) 24
Conan Doyle, Sir Arthur (writer) 146
"conkers" (English game) 154
Constantine (Roman emperor) 100
Corbyn, Jeremy (leader of Labour Party) 122
Cornwall (county in England) 18, 144, 149, 165; Land's End 165; Port Isaac 149
Cornwell, Bernard (writer) 5
Corona virus (COVID-19) 180–183
cricket (sport) 25, 94, 124, 126–132, 145, 158
Cromwell, Oliver (Lord Protector) 107
Crosby-on-Eden (town in Cumbria) 152–153
Cumberland (Duke of) 157
Cumbria (county in England) 48, 57, 62, 109, 115, 134, 138–139, 158, 170, 178, 182
Cutler, Adge (West Country singer) 53

Davies, Hunter (author of *The Living Wall*) 139, 165
Davy, Sir Humphrey (inventor) 24
The Debatable Lands 170
Defoe, Daniel (writer and poet) 87–88
Deutsche Bahn 18
Devon (county in England) 8, 51, 148, 167
Dire Straits (band) 23, 29, 147; *see also* Newcastle
Doomsday (film) 182
Douglas, Kirk (actor) 9; *see also Spartacus*
Dover: Snargate Street 3; Straits of 3; White Cliffs of 3
Dunn, George "Dusty" (pilot) 44
Durham (county and city in England): cathedral 77–78; city of 35

East Anglia (region in England) 18, 107
East India Club (setting in *Around the World in Eighty Days*) 16, 178
Edward I (King of England,"Edward Long-shanks") 157, 171
Elizabeth II (Queen of England) 54
Ely Cathedral 19

England *see* individual place names
English Channel 3, 52, 68, 184
Europa Endlos (song) 19; *see also* Kraftwerk
European Common Market (EEC) 51–53
European Union ("EU") 5, 21–22, 51, 54–57, 70, 169, 182
Exeter (city in Devon) 8, 51–53

Feaver, William (author of *The Pitmen Painters*) 41
Finglandrigg (town in Cumbria) 171
Floyd on France (BBC TV series featuring Keith Floyd) 153
Fogg, Phileas (character in *Around the World in Eighty Days*) 16, 178
food in England 4, 38, 45, 59–61, 79–80, 84, 160, 152–153, 174
football (soccer) 23, 26, 34, 38, 52–53, 56, 81, 124, 150–153

Gallagher, Noel (member of band Oasis) 81
"Geordie" *see* Newcastle
Gibbon, Edward (historian) 66
Gilsland (city in Cumbria) 139–141
Glenridding (town in Cumbria) 138
Glevum or Colonia Nervia Glevensium (Roman city in Britannia) *see* Gloucestershire
global warming 138, 182–183
Gloucestershire (county in England) 74; city of Gloucester 8, 10, 142, 144; Roman city of Glevum 8
Graham, Billy (United States evangelist) 109
Grahame, Kenneth (writer, *The Wind in the Willows*) 69
The Great Recession 51, 125
Great Wall of China 65, 185

Hadrian (Emperor) 16, 65–67, 91, 106, 169, 179
Hadrian's Path *see* individual place names under Hadrian's Wall
Hadrian's Wall: Allabava 171; attacks on 64, 88, 92, 101; Birdsowald 140, 175; Bleat-arn 154–155; Busy Gap 106; Carlisle 5, 16; Carrawburgh 97; Cat Stairs 117–119, 121; Chesters Roman fort 77–78, 84–87; construction of 30, 66–69; ditch (Roman) 64, 72, 101, 150; forts 31, 65, 92, 101, 110; Heavenfield 75–77; Housesteads 31, 94, 106–107, 109–110, 112; Lime-stone Corner 97; ludus latrunculorum (game) 114; milecastles 101–102; Newcastle 36–37; Peel Crags 117; Peel Gap 117, 119; Planetrees 77; reasons for building

68–69; Segedunum museum 30–31; Sewingshields Crags 101; Steel Rigg 112–113, 134–137; Sycamore Gap 116, 118, 135; turrets 65, 85, 101–102; Vallum 64, 72, 140; vici 92; Vindolanda 85, 114; Whin Sill 115, 119, 134, 171

Hadrian's Way 30

Hardy, Thomas (English novelist) 101

Heddon-on-the-Wall 31, 62–64, 70, 72, 78

hedgehog 69–70

Hegel, Friedrich (German philosopher) 185

Hill, Fiona (United States presidential adviser) 182

Homer (Greek author) 91

The Hunger Marches 41

Hutton, William (Hadrian's Wall author) 169–170

Indiana Jones and the Last Crusade (movie) 118

Irish Sea 1, 17, 140

Irthing (river) 68, 139–140, 148

Isca Dumnoniorum (Roman fortress in Britannia) 8

Jackson, Andrew (United States president) 108

Jerusalem (city in Israel) 67

Jerusalem (poem and hymn written by William Blake) 39, 146–147

Johnson, Boris (United Kingdom prime minister) 50, 54, 102

Johnson, Dr. Samuel 169

Julius Caesar (Roman general and dictator) 68, 87

Jumanji (film): 124, 177; Robin Williams 124

Kent (county in England) 3, 87, 101

Kew's Good Wine Shop 15–16; *see also* Ben

Killing Eve (BBC TV series) 16

Kingsnorth, Paul (author of *The Battle Against the Bland*) 49

Klinsmann, Jürgen (German football player and manager) 20

Kraftwerk (band) 19, 125

The Lady from Shanghai (film) 23

Lake District: in Cumbria 16, 35, 138, 156, 175; in Northumberland 115

Lancashire (county in England) 10, 17

Latin (language) 9–11, 30, 32, 64, 68, 89–90

Lemington (town in Northumberland) 39

Levy, Ian (MP from Cumbria) 182

Lindisfarne (Isle of) 115

London: Anglesea Arms pub 81–82;

Chelsea Football Club (F.C.) 39, 81; dominance of 34–35; drunkenness in 123–124; Harry Potter Platform 9¾ Gift Shop 19; Heathrow Airport 18; Kew Gardens 15, 181; King's Cross Station 19; Leadenhall Market 124; Liverpool Street Station 18; living in 22, 27, 46, 49, 50, 69–71, 73, 80–81, 83, 96, 101, 123–126, 133, 144, 147, 153, 166; museums of 5; Paddington Station 18; pubs in 46; Romans in 5, 67, 88; South Kensington 4; train trip to 160, 173–178; 2012 Olympics 5; Victoria Station 18

Longbyre (village in Cumbria) 138

Lord of the Flies (novel by William Golding) 9

Loughborough University 124

Maiden Castle (Dorset) 9

Malcolm, Devon (cricket player) 131–132

Major, Sir John (United Kingdom prime minister) 145, 148

Marcus Aurelius (Roman emperor) 66–67, 179–180

Martin, George R.R. (writer of *A Song of Ice and Fire* and executive producer on *Game of Thrones*) 92–93

RMS *Mauretenia* (ocean liner) 33

May, Theresa (United Kingdom prime minister) 54

McEnroe, John (tennis player) 118

McGoohan, Patrick (actor) 59; *see also The Prisoner*

McManus, Declan ("Elvis Costello," musician) 158, 163

The Midlands (region in England) 107

The Midsomer Murders (BBC TV series) 75, 146, 148

Military Road 71–72, 84, 93, 97, 106, 117, 120

Mithras, Mithraism (mystery religion) 97–100

Montagu Pit Disaster 40–42; statue commemorating 40–41

Nero (Roman emperor) 180

Nerva (Roman emperor) 8, 66

Newbrough (town in Northumberland) 61, 73, 78–79

Newcastle 17, 78, 81, 100, 122, 140, 158; accent 27, 29–30, 45, 48; The Animals (band) 23, 41; *Blaydon Races* 38–39; (Newcastle) Brown Ale 24; cab rides in 26, 30, 159; characteristics of 23–25; drunkenness in 24–25 "Dire Straits 23; "Geordie(s)" 15, 23–24, 26, 30, 124, 139, 181; *Iron Hand* 147; Monopoly (game)

Index

157; Newcastle United F.C. "Magpies" 23, 34, 38, 48; Queen Victoria in 19; religion 63; Roxy Music 23; Sting 23; Swan Hunter shipyard 33; train ride to 15, 19; *Tunnel of Love* 29; Tyne Bridge 58; Tyne River 24, 32, 38; Viz Comics 124

"North Country" 34–35, 45, 116, 139, 163, 182

North Sea 1, 3, 17, 28, 115, 140, 163, 174, 182

Northumberland (county in England) 20, 31, 48, 57, 62, 78, 93, 96, 109, 115, 134, 139, 178

Obama, Barack (United States president) 57

O'Hara, Michael 23; *see also The Lady from Shanghai*

"Old Sparky" (electric chair, Georgia State Prison) 25

Once Brewed (town in Northumberland) *see* Twice Brewed

Orwell, George (writer of *Road to Wigan Pier*) 40, 83

Paradise Lost (poem by John Milton) 146

Pelosi, Nancy (United States Speaker of the House of Representatives) 102

Pennines (mountain chain in England) 96

Penrith (town in Cumbria) 170

Picts (people) 6, 88, 151, 157

Pink Floyd (band) 153

Polk, James Knox (United States President) 108

Port Carlisle (town in Cumbria) 171–172

The Prisoner (TV series) 59

The Proclaimers (Scottish band) 20

Pubs: closures of 49–50; 144, 172; *Good Pub Guide* 49; music 152

"Puffing Billy" (steam locomotive) 43

"Quakers" (Society of Friends) 106

Rackham, Oliver (writer) 146

Reagan, Ronald (United States President) 109

Realm magazine (since renamed *Discover Britain*) 35

Red Lion Inn *see* Newbrough

Red Rock Fault 139–140

red squirrel 69

Reeves and Mortimer (BBC TV sketch) 24

"reivers" 106, 170; William Faulkner novel, *The Reivers* 106

The Revolutionary War 109; Cowpens, Battle of 109

Robert the Bruce 171

Robin Hood Inn (pub in Northumberland) 73

Robin Hood: Prince of Thieves (film) 116

rock formations: dolerite 115; limestone 36, 64, 77–78, 96–97, 115, 140, 142; sandstone 77, 115

Roman Army: Asturians in (Spanish) 87; auxiliaries 69, 85–87, 91–92, 97, 99, 109, 140; centurion 30–31, 68, 90–91; century 90–91; cohort 90–91, 112; construction of bridge over Rhine River 69; contubernium 90; Dacians in (Romanians) 87, 140; Dalmatians in (Croatians) 87; Ethiopians in 171; Frisians in 171; Iraqis in 87; Legio II Augusta (II Legion) 9, 109; Legio IX Hispana (IX Legion) 68; Moroccans in 171; life of soldiers in Britain 84–89; principia 110, 171; Syrians in 87; Tungrians in (Belgians) 85, 111; uniforms, tactics, and equipment of 89–90; weapons of 90; *see also* Romans in London

Romans in Britain: baths 84, 88; Christianity in 76, 100, 114; contributions 11–12, 184; food 86; trade with 87; wine and beer 86–87

Roosevelt, Theodore (United States President) 109

Roxy Music (band) 23; *see also* Newcastle

rugby (sport): 43, 62, 123–124, 128, 142; British Lions 25; Calcutta Cup (Scotland vs. England rugby) 19–20; Murrayfield Stadium 20; Six Nations Championship 20; song *Swing Low* 39, 146; World Cup 22, 178

Scotland: Annan 166–167; Ben Lomond 16; Berwick Upon Tweed 20, 157; Edinburgh 14, 19, 21, 52, 96, 157, 168–169; Galashiels 106; Glasgow 168–169; Gretna 168; Hawick 168; Highlands 16; Inverness 72; Scots (language) 103, 151; Scots (people) 6, 20, 72, 150–151, 167, 169, 170–171, 182; Scottish National Party 21

Scots-Irish (people) 108–109

Scotswood (town in Northumberland) 40

Septimius Severus (emperor) 91–92

Shakespeare, William (Roman history plays) 10

Shearer, Alan (England footballer) 34

Sherpa Expeditions ("Sherpas") 28, 120, 136–137, 141–143, 161

Smallpox (in Roman Empire) 179–180

Softball (sport) 126–128

Solway Firth 164–165, 171

South Africa: Durban (cricket) 25; Lords (cricket) 130–132

Spartacus (film) 9

The Spectator (British magazine) 81
The Spice Girls (band) 4
Spooky Tooth (band) 150; *see also* Carlisle
The Stag's Inn (pub in Crosby-on-Eden) 152–153
Steele, James (musician and poet) 147–148
Stephenson, George (engineer) 24, 43
Sting (musician) 23; *see also* Newcastle
Storm Desmond 137–138
Storm Eva 138
Strabo (Greek historian) 86
Sunderland (city in Durham) 15–16

Talking Heads (band) 102
The Teardrop Explodes (band) 118
Thatcher, Margaret (United Kingdom Prime Minister) 41
Thirlwall Castle 138
Thompson, Emma (actress) 81
"Three Tenors" (Placido Domingo, Jose Carreras, Luciano Pavarotti) 13
Tolkien, J.R.R. (author of *Lord of the Rings* trilogy) 115
Trainspotting (film) 81
Trajan (Roman emperor) 65–66, 106
Trans Europa Express (song) 19; *see also* Kraftwerk
Trump, Donald (United States President) 5, 29, 57, 80, 102, 109, 182–183
Twice Brewed (town in Northumberland): Inn 118, 122–132; Vallum Lodge 117, 120–122, 132–135, 139, 145; village 85, 117, 119
Typhoon Hagibis (Japan) 177
Tyrolean Alps 19

University of Cumbria 158
University of Durham 123
University of Newcastle 24

Valencia, Spain: Mestalla Stadium 10–11, 13; Valencia CF 10; vomitorio 11, 13
Valentinian (Roman emperor) 88
Varro (Roman writer) 114
Vespasian (Roman general and emperor) 9
Virginia (Chesapeake Bay) 107

Wales 6, 28, 59, 101
Wallsend (town in Northumberland) 29–30, 33, 142
Walton (town in Cumbria) 134, 136, 141, 144, 147–148, 175; Low Rigg Bed and Breakfast 142–145
Warren, C. Henry (writer) 146
Welles, Orson 23; *see also The Lady from Shanghai*
Wesley, John (co-founder of Methodism) 63
Western, Harry (World War I soldier) 71
Whitley Bay (town in Northumberland): "Jerry" 28–30; The Lighthouse (bed and breakfast) 28; Spanish City 29; Turknaz (restaurant) 28
Whyte, Jack (writer) 5
The Wicker Man (film) 165
William I ("The Conqueror—King of England) 101
Wilmot, Aimee (daughter of co-author, David) 123
Wilmot, Calum (son of co-author, David) 122, 176–177
Wilmot, Kirstie (daughter of co-author, David) 122
Wilson, Woodrow (United States President) 109, 158
World War I ("The Great War") 43–44, 71, 159
World War II 9, 58, 70–71, 146, 180–181
Wylam (town in Northumberland) 33, 38, 43–45, 47, 54, 58–61, 63, 82, 175; Boathouse Pub 47–58; Cenotaph (World War I memorial) 43–44; during World War II 58; Fox and Hounds Pub 45–48; Waggonway 43; Wormald House 45–47, 59–61

Yorkshire (county in England) 4, 17, 35, 45, 52, 64, 79, 131, 171; Dales 4, 35; pudding 45, 79
Yourcenar, Marguerite (writer of *Memoirs of Hadrian*) 66